D1571714

# GERMAN VEHICLES IN WORLD WAR II
# *Volkswagens of the Wehrmacht*
## *A Photo Chronicle*

## Hans-Georg Mayer-Stein

**Schiffer Military History**
Atglen, PA

# Bibliography

## Books:

Boschen, Lothar, Das grosse Buch der Volkswagen-Typen, Stuttgart 1983.
Domarus, Max, Hitler-Reden 1932 bis 1945, Munich 1965.
Eichler, Max, Du bist sofort im Bilde, Reichsbürger-Handbuch, Erfurt 1939.
Etzold, Hans-Rüdiger, Der Käfer II, Stuttgart 1984.
Macho, Engelbert, Der VW-Schwimmwagen Typ 128, Maria-Enzersdorf bei Wien 1966.
Müller, Jens-Theo, & Eiken, Hermann, Der VW-Bus, Wiesbaden 1988.
Oswald, Werner, Kraftfahrzeuge und Panzer der Reichswehr, Wehrmacht und Bundeswehr, Stuttgart 1973.
Picker, Henry, & Hoffmann, Heinrich, Hitlers Tischgespräche im Bild, Munich/Berlin 1980.
Piekalkiewicz, Janusz, Der VW Kübelwagen Typ 82 im Zweiten Weltkrieg, Stuttgart 1977.
Sabatés, Fabien, Der Käfer, Geneva, no date.
Spielberger, Walter J., Die Motorisierung der Deutschen Reichswehr 1920-1935, Stuttgart 1979.

## Periodicals:

Das Auto, Motor und Sport, Freiburg im Breisgau, 1946 to 1948.
Automobil-Chronik, 6/72, 11/74, 4/75, 2/77, 10/77, 12/77, 5/79, 8/79, 3/80.
Der Spiegel, Vol. 4, No. 18, Special Brochure (published by Volkswagenwerk, June 1950).

Translated from the German by Dr. Edward Force.

This book was originally published under the title,
*Volkswagen Militärfahrzeuge 1938-1948,*
by Podzun-Pallas Verlag.

Copyright © 1994 by Schiffer Publishing Ltd.
Library of Congress Catalog Number: 94-66972

Printed in the United States of America.
ISBN: 0-88740-684-X

We are interested in hearing from authors with book ideas on related topics.

Published by Schiffer Publishing Ltd.
77 Lower Valley Road
Atglen, PA 19310
Please write for a free catalog.
This book may be purchased from the publisher.
Please include $2.95 postage.
Try your bookstore first.

# CONTENTS

Foreword                                                      5
The Volkswagen Concept                                        6
The KdF-Wagen of 1938                                        12
Kübelwagen Before World War II                               22
Personnel Cars and Motorcycles of the Wehrmacht             25
The Volkswagen as a Military Vehicle                         27
   Kübelwagen                                 27
   Schwimmwagen                               28
   VW Beetle                                  29
   Types and Development Numbers              30
Running on Wood Gas                                          68
The Volkswagen in Action                                     77
Wolfsburg 1945-1946                                         136
   List of Types                             141
Postwar Driving                                             154
Privately Owned Wehrmacht Volkswagens                       157

# Foreword

Transportation has always played a decisive role in the development of human civilization and culture, as well as determining their decline or destruction. Thus the available means of transportation have always been made available for peaceful and warlike purposes. Means of transportation have always been expressions of individual and collective capabilities or mentalities, of civilizing potentialities and formative abilities of a time, epoch, nation or people, as well as the unrest of man, his aggressive potential or desire to assert himself.

The automobile, which made motorized individual transit possible and revolutionized mass transport, gives evidence of this to the highest degree. Illustrating this in a segment of history is the purpose of this book.

The technical development of the automobiles presented here – the VW Beetle, Kübel- and Schwimmwagen – has often been described and will not be repeated here. To the purist, this material is already know in great detail. Thus the listing of technical details and chronological dates will be dispensed with.

Instead, this book, in words and pictures, shows historical technology in connection with the people who had to operate with it. Thus it documents a piece of German everyday history. Avoiding military-technical books as a matter of principle would therefore be ignoring something that is a part of our national history and existence.

The author thanks all those who willingly contributed information and pictures that helped to make this book a success, including Siegfried Bunke (Duisburg), Peter Ebeling (Berlin), Eduard Knoll (Lorch, Württemberg), Jürgen Knolle (Braunschweig), Engelbert Macho (Maria Enzersdorf near Vienna), Vladimir Marsik (Prague), Carsten Messer (Braunschweig), Dr. Ulrich von Pidoll (Braunschweig), Hermann Rest (Ostfildern near Stuttgart, of the periodical "Gute Fahrt"), Jürgen Schultz (Memmingen), and particularly Gunter and Norbert Schwefer (Bielefeld).

The VW Museum in Wolfsburg (Dr. Bernd Wiersch and Ms. Resow). the Porsche Archives in Stuttgart-Zuffenhausen (Mr. Klaus Parr and Ms. Jopp), the Federal Archives in Koblenz and the Bavarian State Library in Munich have also been kind enough to make pictures available.

Finally, thanks are also due to Mr. Roland Fränkle (Karlsruhe) for his kind assistance in the reproduction of photos and the restoration of a Kübelwagen.

The Author
Karlsruhe, Autumn 1993

# The Volkswagen Principle

The automobile was originally a means of transportation for the rich. Remarkably, though, shortly after the turn of the century there were attempts made to create a small car for everyone. The 4 HP Lilliput of the Bergmann Industriewerke in Gaggenau near Rastatt, Baden (today Unimog), was a first attempt in its time (1904-1907). It was meant to cost 2500 Marks and was therefore scarcely attainable by the average wage-earner.

The automobile attained its first significance as a means of mass transport in World War I, when trucks in particular were utilized for supplying and moving troops to the western front. Thus the automobile gained its operative importance for the first time.

In the Weimar Republic, automobile fever really got into full swing for the first time in Germany. People were intoxicated by the fantasies of endless streams of traffic, cities built for auto traffic and individual motorization with the auto for everyone.

And yet: In the 1920s, general motorization was able to proceed only slowly in Germany. To be sure, there were a whole series of very promising technical developments and imaginative new designs, but the deliberate enthusiasm, the most stubborn activism and the most zealous efforts almost all came to grief under the pressure of the tremendous economic crises. The number of firms that failed is vast. After World War I, Germany had grown smaller and poorer. The economic sacrifices were enormous. The German heavy industry, which had provided the basis for quick economic progress in the preceding years, was shaken and seriously threatened. According to the demands of the victorious powers, Germany had lost its merchant fleet and its international investments of capital, and thus the earning power of its shipping and the profits and interest flowing in from countries to the west. Since a great portion of Germany's stocks of railroad equipment and motor vehicles had to be surrendered, transportation had also had to endure a serious setback. In addition, the Entente demanded high reparations. Under the ever more stringent conditions, economic reconstruction was possible only under the greatest effort, and the Weimar Republic enjoyed economic prosperity in the latter half of the 1920s only for a short time, on the unsteady basis of short-term foreign credit.

It is no surprise that, under these conditions, the German Reich, in terms of automobile production, ranked in last place among the industrial nations of the West. The automobile was not yet a means of mass transit in Europe – unlike in the USA, where Henry Ford had long since made the Model T a widespread people's car. In Germany in the mid-1920s, about half of public street transit was still supplied by horse-drawn wagons. Thus a great part of the transit system was still dominated by the power of the horse. The motor car was still regarded as a luxury item, and was thus burdened with a special tax by the state. And above all else, the network of roads in the German Reich was in no way suited to auto travel. World War I had shattered many plans. And after that, the money was lacking. The construction of special auto roads was still in its beginning stage. Unpaved dusty roads that turned into seas of mud were the bane of the driver's existence. A quick advance here was not possible. The years of inflation, the economic collapse, the unemployment, the world economic crisis placed heavy burdens on Germany.

And yet: In the Germany of the 1920s, the trend toward the car for everyman, the small car – which, admittedly, not every man could afford for some time to come – was developing. But the possession of a car was no longer supposed to be a privilege of the well-to-do upper class, as it was before World War I. Soon after 1918 there appeared, through the courage of improvisation, a number of small vehicles to mobilize the common people. At first they popped up out of the ground like mushrooms. But the country's growing financial troubles quickly brought many courageous strivings to an end, and the small cars disappeared into the darkness of history as quickly as their names, and not long after their more or less noteworthy end there were only a few people who still remembered the vanished small cars, which often had been made in very small numbers and distributed only locally or regionally: Alan, Hataz, Eos, Nug, Ipe, Mops, Maryette, Atlantic, Gridi, York, Bully, Bravo. Rikas, Peer Gynt, Walmobil, Bob, Diana, to mention just a few exotic names. They were all forgotten, and very little is known of their brief existence.

The economic recovery that resulted from an influx of American capital led to a growing index of production and a growing gross national product after 1925. Success came to the automobile business as well. The hectic, restless times of the 1920s came very close to attaining general motorization. Toward the end of the 1920s, the cars for the people became sturdier, better developed and capable of being taken more seriously for everyday use than the lightweights of the 1920-1924 period. For example, there were the NSU 5/25, the renowned Dixi, the DKW P 15 PS and Front types, the Hanomag Kommissbrot or 3/16, the Opel 7.34 and 8/40. They all appeared to be the stuff of reasonably priced people's cars, although there had been very proper, popular cars of the type before, such as the Wanderer Puppchen.

But the German automobile industry had to struggle against tough American competition, after the government, on October 1, 1925, had lifted import restrictions on foreign motor vehicles and reduced customs duties on them. The reason for these measures can be found in the Dawes Plan (named after its initiator, Charles Dawes, the director of the Morgan Bank), which provided the German economy with a total credit of 800 million dollars, intended to bring an end to inflation and assure German reparations payments. The American investments in German industry – in Thyssen, AEG, Krupp, Siemens & Halske, the German chemical, petroleum and rubber industries – were not altruistic. The Automotive Product AG had been founded in Berlin in 1920, with both General Motors and Ford belonging to it. In 1925 Ford built an assembly plant in the Westhafen district of Berlin and turned out its famous Model T there, which had been built by the millions in the USA and contributed to full motorization there. With its low prices, made possible by modern mass production, Ford could drive its German competitors out of the field, for with their outmoded production methods they could not stand up to the American frontal attack. The Model A Ford, which succeeded the Model T in 1928, was considerably cheaper than any comparable German car. America was synonymous with technical progress, and the mass culture with its American Way of Life conquered the big cities of Germany.

When the world economic crisis suddenly broke into Germany in 1929, German automobile production dropped by almost two thirds. In the great depression, the German dream of a car for everyone was impossible for the time being. Only Jörgen Rasmussen, Josef Ganz and Ferdinand Porsche had hopes for the future of a German people's car. The example of the Model T Ford in America was their model. Other foreign manufacturers had also tried to popularize the reasonably priced and utilitarian people's car already. Hans Ledwinka tried his luck with a small Tatra, Austin with the Austin Seven, which was built since 1922 and also built under license by the Dixi Works in Eisenach since 1927, Citroen with the 5 CV, and Opel with its "Laubfrosch", a copy of the Citroen two-seater.

Jörgen Skafte Rasmussen, who came from Denmark, had moved to Saxony before World War I and built electric and steam cars during the war, at the Zschopauer Armaturenfabrik which he had founded. Rasmussen, filled with an unquenchable urge to plan, was able to expand his factory methodically into a far-flung organization: he was a tireless purchaser of designs, patents, stocks, production facilities and subcontractors. In 1928 the Zschoppauer Motorenwerke J.S. Rasmussen AG had become the world's largest motorcycle factory. After buying the firm of Audi, Rasmussen made his name as an auto manufacturer in 1928 by producing an eight-cylinder Audi. This fine car brought him no luck in the economic crisis, but his DKW Front, which had been designed by the Audi design office and built since 1931, became a sales success. In the technical world, the little DKW was praised to the skies, and the interested public was fascinated by the car, which cost only 1750 Reichsmark in roadster form. Within four years, 100,000 DKW's had rolled off the assembly line, and thus the car had become a mass-produced article in Germany.

To a certain extent, Rasmussen had thus attained what had been in the minds of the German car builders since the start of the 1920s.

The people's-car idea also received much support from Josef Ganz, the publisher of the "Motor-Kritik." The factory promoted the Superior, developed for production as of 1933 by the Standard-Werke in Ludwigsburg, founded by Wilhelm Gutbrod in 1926, as a "German People's Car." The Superior anticipated certain design elements of the later Volkswagen Beetle: rear engine, central tubular frame and streamlined body. These elements are also found in Ledwinka's Tatra and the rear-engine Mercedes. Great success, of course, could not be gained by Ganz's Standard, for it was too much a product of the economic crisis: the car had a weak motor (396 cc, 12 HP), offered far too little space (only two narrow seats), and looked rather pathetic (wooden body with just two side windows). The car was also extremely overpriced at 1590 Reichsmark, for a full-grown 1.2-liter Opel cost only 300 RM more. In addition, Gutbrod had too little production capacity in his factory, which moved to Stuttgart-Feuerbach in 1933 and Plochingen in 1937.

Thus only about 300 of the Standard Superior 400 were sold between 1933 and 1935, and even an improved version, the Superior 500, could not attain better sales figures.

Hitler's rise to power brought about the decisive change in the People's-Car project, since it was sanctioned by the government from then on. On February 11, 1933, at the opening of the International Automobile and Motorcycle Exhibition on the Kaiserdamm in Berlin, the new Reich

Chancellor energetically supported the advancement of auto traffic and advocated "gradual tax reductions, introduction and carrying out of a large-scale roadbuilding plan, advancement of sporting events." As for the automobile industry, Hitler favored the right impetus to push the design of a People's Car, which was amplified by the fact that he was fascinated by automobiles.

The decisiveness with which the new government carried out the motorization program is only one facet of those all-encompassing measures that resulted in a quick reduction in unemployment, as well as a rigid, totalitarian penetration of all areas of life. In charge of the motorization of the Third Reich was the Nationalsozialistische Kraftfahrkorps (NSKK), a formation of the SA, founded in 1931 and under the direction of Adolf Hühnlein of Chemnitz. The NSKK promoted free driver training and organized countless motor sport events. The government also sought prestige in auto racing, for sensational victories on the racecourse promised the state more than increased international prestige. The effective advertising and exciting aura of auto racing were part of the arsenal of the ingenious Nazi propaganda technique.

The building of the Autobahn system was part of the regime's spectacular undertakings. The original planned length of 6900 kilometers was extended to 14,000 in the Greater German Reich. By the time the war began, 4000 kilometers had been finished. The mighty construction program that was carried out here was viewed as proof of both the economic potential for achievement and the commercial success that the regime could display, supported by a rising worldwide upswing. The improvement of the automobile market was brought on by a series of tax breaks, such as the absence of taxes on new vehicles in a unique installment plan. The promotion of auto traffic was thus pushed with the same sort of pressure as the increase in air traffic or the motorization of army units, and the prosperity that soon made itself known here was brought into the spotlight with full propaganda effect.

In 1933 there were 755,156 motor vehicles (cars, trucks and buses) in the German Reich; in 1938 there were about a million more. An astonishing growth rate can also be seen in motorcycle construction: 844,042 motorcycles in 1933, 1,599,055 in 1938. With 200,000 units produced, 63% of the world's yearly motorcycle production came from Germany. The growth rate exceeded all expectations and showed the potential of a total motorization program: "The motor vehicle production will reach its high point after the completion of the KdF-Wagen factory in Fallersleben, the largest in the world. The KdF-Wagen, designed by Dr. Porsche, costs 990 RM and will fulfill the wishes of hundreds of thousands of Volksgenossen for a motor car." (Eichler, p. 184)

The fact that the Volkswagen concept was realized with state support was based on Hitler's personal initiative, for he promoted the project with his typical determination. In 1934 he had already stated, in his own socialistic tenor, with which the Nazi Party sought the favor of the working class: "It is a bitter feeling that millions of good, hardworking people have known that they were excluded from using an instrument of travel that would have been a source of an unknown, joyful happiness, especially on Sundays and holidays. One must have the courage to attack this problem with determination and in a big way. What cannot be achieved in one year will – perhaps – be accepted as an obvious fact in ten years."(quoted from "Der Spiegel", Vol.IV, No.18, special issue). And on March 7, 1934, again at the opening of the International Automobile Exhibition in Berlin, Hitler stated, among other things: "If we really want to increase the numbers of automobile owners in Germany into the millions, then this can only succeed when we make its price fit the financial level of the millions of buyers under consideration. If the German government wishes the German people to take an active share in the automobile, then the industry must create and build the suitable automobiles for the German people. Just a few months ago German industry succeeded, by producing a new people's radio set, in putting on the market and selling an enormous number of radios. I would now like to make it the most important mission of the German motor vehicle industry to build more and more of the car that necessarily opens to it a level of millions of new buyers, for only when we succeed in conquering the greatest masses for this new means of transportation will not only the economic but also the social good be indisputable." (Domarus, p. 370)

Beyond a doubt, the influence of the dictator prepared the prerequisites for the realization of the Volkswagen project. The totalitarian state could provide the means that were needed for planning, testing and producing it. The prelude to the Volkswagen story, from the first designs in 1934 to the display of the KdF-Wagen and the laying of the factory cornerstone in 1938, has often been described (for example, by Boschen, Etzold or Müller and Eicken), so that we can sum it up briefly here: As of 1934, all the planning was in the hands of the design office of Ferdinand Porsche, whose career included all the prerequisites for governmental support.

Porsche, born in Reichenberg in the Sudetenland in 1875, began his career at the United Electric Company in Vienna in 1894, after having drawn attention to himself by his electro-technical finesse. His positions took them then from his job as a designer for the Imperial and Royal court producer Ludwig Lohner in Vienna-Florisdorf, where he gained renown from the gasoline-electric Lohner Porsche Mischwagen, to the Austro-Daimler AG in 1905. There Porsche built his first gasoline motor car, as well as aircraft motors. He won fame with a racing car of his own design in the Prince Heinrich Trials of 1907 and 1910, which were sponsored by Prince Heinrich, a brother of Kaiser Wilhelm and a passionate motorist, and which thus promoted the automobile in the name of the imperial house. For the Skoda Works in Pilsen, Porsche developed various means of transporting the heaviest loads (motorized military mortars, gasoline-electric towing tractors).

His achievements in the technology of Austrian military motorization brought him – he had meanwhile become the General Manager of the Austro-Daimler Works – an honorary doctorate from the Technische Hochschule in Vienna.

After World War I, Porsche, following the general trend, turned to the design of utilitarian vehicles. In 1923, leaving Austro-Daimler after a disagreement, he moved to Daimler Motoren AG in Stuttgart-Untertürkheim and attained an executive position. With the supercharged two-liter car he developed, Christian Werner was able to win the 1924 Targa Florio race. The renowned supercharged 6-cylinder S, SS and SSK, as powerful as they were aesthetic, also stand to Porsche's credit. Permanent animosities, of which Porsche's choleric temperament was not blameless, brought an end to his collaboration with Daimler-Benz in 1929. After a brief term with Steyr, he finally set up his own design bureau in Stuttgart and worked under contract for foreign car builders, similarly to the present-day Porsche Development Center in Weisach.

After the Volkswagen planning had been promoted in a big way by the government, and especially by Hitler himself, Porsche recommended himself with references to his successful previous activities and his neutral design office, which was not linked to the commercial interests of any firm. The first step to cooperation with the state had already been made when Porsche had received state support in the design of a racing car. His long-standing close relationship to Jakob Werlin, chief of Daimler-Benz and an admirer, compatriot and automotive advisor of Adolf Hitler since the early days, may also have helped Porsche to make a sensation. Perhaps Hitler also saw Porsche as the brilliant realizer of extraordinary ideas, and perhaps also the deep-rotted mistrust of Hitler, who had risen from the bottom, toward people with bourgeois origins that made him prefer the self-taught outsider of Bohemian-Austrian origins – the dictator may well have sensed that Porsche was a kindred spirit.

The birth of the Volkswagen is generally dated according to the famous "Exposé concerning the construction of a German People's Car" that Porsche wrote and submitted to the Reich Transport Ministry on January 17, 1934. In it, Porsche summed up his technical and economic concepts in five points. On the basis of these concepts, the Reichsverband der Automobil-Industrie issued a contract for the construction of a prototype of the future Volkswagen. The Exposé had already included the framework for the technical concept: air-cooling, rear engine, swing axle, rear-wheel drive, torsion-bar suspension were all envisioned. The traditional frame construction with bodywork set on it and screwed to it was to make various body types possible.

The years of incubation, in which the Volkswagen grew out of the design plans and took shape, lasted from 1934 to 1938. Porsche's quarrels with the automobile industry are all too understandable given the thousand impossibilities that now became obvious: The project consumed far more money than had been planned, Porsche could come nowhere near adhering to the time span called for by the contract, and in addition, the German auto manufacturers were absolutely not interested in supporting a future competitor. A further problem was that the selling price called for by Hitler was not to be more than 1000 Marks. The calculatory finesse finally resulted in the well-known VW savings system, which was organized by the German Workers' Front, a kind of unionized amalgamation into which the former commercial organizations were also integrated. The DAF, divided into specialized offices and units and directed by Dr. Robert Ley, was, to be sure, also in charge of the National Socialist "Kraft durch Freude" organization, which developed a series of sociopolitical activities that made the regime remarkably popular, such as tours, cruises, sporting events and a people's education system, and which now was to take over the distribution of the Volkswagen so as to save the dealers' commissions – to keep the final price as low as possible.

Prototypes of the Volkswagen were shown to the public beginning in 1936, while they were on the way to test runs (often in the Black forest or the Alps). The test vehicles, which were nothing to look at, were subjected to tests developed by the SS-Fahrbereitschaft. In 1938 the volkswagen assumed its final form and was presented to the German public on Ascension Day of the same year, May 26, when Adolf Hitler laid the cornerstone of the factory.

Wolfsburg was planned as a great production city, with modern housing projects, green areas, streets of stores, strips of park, main traffic routes and boulevards, great squares, theaters, auditoriums, impressive National Socialist buildings, and naturally Autobahn and canal connections as well. The plans called for 15,000 Morgens of land. The work was carried on with all possible hectic haste. The first apartment buildings were ready in March of 1938. The workers were housed in a big common dormitory – under conditions that seem Spartan by present-day standards, but which inspired euphoric optimism at the time after years of mass unemployment. In mid-September, 2400 Italians came to replace German workers who had been ordered to work on the West Wall – a clear sign of a coming war on Germany's part. The Third Reich propagandized the German-Italian friendship. The Tullio-Cianetti Hall, named after the president of the Fascist worker's organization in Italy, who laid its cornerstone along with Robert Ley on June 27, 1938, was built for organized group leisure activities.

In all parts of the Greater German Reich, from Baden to East Prussia, work forces were recruited, including in the former Austria and Sudetenland. 2358 apartments had been occupied. In December 1941, though, the Nazi government halted all work on the KdF city. The building of new German cities was no longer important to the war effort.

# The KdF-Wagen of 1938

The prototype of the Volkswagen (VW/Porsche Type 60) was nowhere near as original and modern as one often thinks in retrospect today: central tube frames, air-cooled opposed engines, rear engines, independent suspension and streamlined bodywork were all design features of numerous cars already in the 1920s. Thus Porsche did not invent the VW design as completely new, but cleverly combined ideas and components that were in vogue. This, of course, does not diminish his achievement.

Porsche took the central tubular frame from Hans Ledwinka, his Bohemian compatriot, who had used it effectively in the Tatra.

Even the beetle shape of the VW, so beloved today, was not as original and modern as is often thought. In the 1920s, the Viennese Paul Jaray (1889-1974) had already made a name for himself as a pioneer in aerodynamics and streamlining. Jaray had studied at the Technische Hochschule in Prague and had then worked in the aircraft industry for a time before he turned to designing automobile bodies. He worked for such well-known manufacturers as Adler, Alfa Romeo, Audi, Fiat, Hanomag, Mercedes-Benz, Maybach, Peugeot, Skoda, Steyr and Tatra. His best-known design in Germany was the Adler "Autobahn" type.

In car-crazy America, a Jaray Streamline Corporation was even founded and tried to sell licenses. Chrysler and Ford did take up Jaray's ideas, though without bothering about his rights. Along with Vienna's Paul Jaray, Edmund Rumpler (1872-1940) also became known for his famous "teardrop" car, a highly futuristic vehicle that was developed after wind-tunnel experiments.

The advantages of streamlining were obvious: less air resistance, lower fuel consumption, higher speed, less dirtying of the car, easy cleaning, optimal space utilization (no unnecessary running boards), better ventilation, practical production, etc. In terms of saving space, it was only reasonable to put the motor of a streamlined car in the back. This was also done with the Mercedes 130 H and 170 H, or the big Tatra 603. The Volkswagen, with its flat boxer motor, went one step further in this direction.

A modern all-steel body (without the traditional wooden body, as still found in the DKW) had been chosen for the VW from the start, for it offered the desired advantage of practical production in the American way, by connecting the few body parts by simple spot welding. The outer parts – fenders, running boards, bumpers –were screwed on and thus easy to replace in case of accidents. But the body was still set on a chassis and screwed onto the frame in the traditional way. The new Opel Olympia of 1936 had pointed the way to the modern self-supporting body. The traditional construction of the VW did, of course, provide the highest stability and made it possible to change bodies quickly; thus it was cost-intensive and did its part to phase the "Beetle" out in the midseventies. With its old frame construction, the most often-built German car at that point was an automotive fossil.

When the cornerstone of the VW factory was laid in 1938, three body types of the KdF-Wagen were displayed: limousine, cabrio-limousine and cabriolet.

The VW had its well-known four-cylinder opposed motor. Yet Porsche was not committed to this concept from the beginning. He also experimented with two-cylinder, two-stroke motors, which had proved to be remarkably inexpensive to run in the DKW cars of the mid-1930s and were cheap to produce.

For the Volkswagen, though, which according to government specifications had to be "Autobahnsure", the two-stroke concept proved to be of little use from the beginning. Franz Reimspiess, who carried out engine development in the Porsche design bureau, suggested the new approach with the air-cooled boxer motor.

During his technical career, Porsche had had much experience with this type of motor. He himself had developed an air-cooled four-cylinder boxer motor for Austro-Daimler in 1912-13. This design was in vogue; numerous planning bureaus were working on it, with varying success. But the advantages of the air-cooled boxer were clear: a sturdy crankshaft because of its short length, good weight distribution, little need of space and a low center of gravity, low weight (decreased even more by using light metal), practical, low-cost production (scarcely more costly than a two-stroke). A further advantage: The flat form of the engine block was especially well suited to installation in the rear of the streamlined body. The combination of motor, gearbox and differential resulted in a compact powerplant. But this typical VW powerplant design, which was still used in the VW 411/412 until the mid-seventies, and even in the third-generation VW Bus (as of 1979), was not an original invention of the Porsche Design Bureau, but goes back to a drawing made by designer Bela Berenyi in 1926 and was first used by Hanomag in a 1926 experimental vehicle.

The VW motor in its original version displaced only 985 cc and produced 23.5 HP. As of March 1943, the more powerful motor of the Schwimmwagen (1131 cc, 24.5 HP) was installed in all Volkswagens. That may seem like a very small change today, but at that time other cars of that class had no more. The proverbial long lifetime of the VW motor, at least until about 1960, had its origin in the low value of the specific piston travel, that which resulted on the road, for the VW was conceived from the start as a short-stroke engine. At a time when motors had to be overhauled after 40,000 to 50,000 kilometers as a rule, the Volkswagen could reach at least 100,000.

Whoever has a chance today of switching from a modern small car to an older standard-shift VW, or even a KdF-Wagen – if only for a test ride – will be sadly disappointed and regard the car as a bad dream.

The suspension of the original VW was stiff and scarcely damped. How must its poor performance have felt in those days on the hard cobblestone streets, or the roads that were still unpaved in many places!

It is no wonder that the Americans, accustomed to comfort, who examined the VW after the war did not think highly of it. The improved suspension of the Beetle that drew praise in later test reports was the result of years of laborious work on details. On the other hand, the VW had independent suspension from the start, which was only found in high-priced cars otherwise, and thus it was more pleasant to drive on the bad roads of the 1930s and 1940s than the widespread cars with simple rigid axles.

All VW drivers will still remember the singing and howling gearbox. The unsynchronized gears (with integrated differential) required a lot of skill and sensitivity: Between declutching and clutching, depending on the engine speed and running temperature, more or less (and finely dosed!) gas had to be given. Whoever has driven a standard-shift VW built in or before 1964 will remember the laborious use of the gas pedal from sad experience. Shifting between third and fourth gears was completely problem-free, but in the lower gears, even the most experienced driver could have problems. In addition, the unsynchronized gearbox was clearly inferior when one had to shift quickly: in heavy city traffic, when climbing or making sharp turns on mountain roads. To be sure, experiments with synchronization, double-clutching and automatic transmission were already being carried out by the Porsche staff in 1938-1940.

In its original form, the Volkswagen had mechanical (cable) brakes, which required heavy pedal pressure from the driver. In the more refined export model, which was introduced in 1949, the change was soon made, in May of 1950, to hydraulic brakes, which operated more smoothly and evenly. The simple standard-shift VW, to the horror of many VW owners, retained its antiquated cable brakes until April 1962. The high pedal pressure and pulling to the left or right (even with well-adjusted brakes) caused the owners a lot of annoyance.

The cable brakes, though, were better than their reputation: If the cables were well maintained, regularly greased and adjusted, they worked quite well. For after all, the original standard Beetle, as well as the old Kübel- and Schwimmwagen, were driven until well into the sixties, often even with a trailer, and used by many people for vacation trips to Bavaria, Tyrol or the like: downhill in second gear with the motor's braking effect and the driver's foot solidly on the brake pedal. The somewhat difficult spindle steering too, not without play, was not exactly a source of pure joy. In addition, when driving over railroad crossings or on cobblestone streets, the heavy shocks to the steering made one aware that a steering damper was lacking.

In short, measured by today's standards, the Volkswagen was meager and poorly equipped, uncomfortably upholstered, poorly sprung, with a terrible gearbox, mediocre brakes and a weak motor.

As a low-priced economy car for everyone, the KdF-Wagen was a considerable achievement for 1938 – equal to its competitors, if not superior to them in many ways, and unlike the other small cars of those days, a real car with plenty of room, a sufficiently powerful motor, extraordinarily well-developed and economical, with an air of ruggedness: in the first years of individual driving it was a utilitarian vehicle of the greatest practicality. In addition, the VW was never ranked as a small car from the start; it never gave the impression of being undersize. The bodywork was perfectly formed, and the people's car had a timeless style.

The Nazi advertising portrayed the Volkswagen as a car for work and spare time: for the occasional weekend drive, and for agricultural use as a beast of burden with luggage rack and trailer. At the calculated large-scale production, the price of 990 Reichsmark would have been quite realistic (in comparison, the Opel Kadett cost 2100 RM, the DKW Meisterklasse 2350 RM, the Ford Taunus 2870 RM, the Adler Triumph Junior 2950 RM).

After the cornerstone of the VW factory near Fallersleben was laid, the KdF-Wagen was displayed in many German cities and advertised in brochures, pamphlets and periodicals. The state-promoted savings system was in full operation. From 1930 to 1940, 54 KdF-Wagen and six cabrios were built. On August 15, 1940, the first saleable VW left the factory. Series production began on July 11, 1941 and official delivery on September 3. The production of the limousine was ended by war conditions on August 17, 1944. 630 closed and 13 open KdF-Wagen had been built by then (not counting off-road sedans). Most of these vehicles went to agencies of the party or state, or to factory staff.

The VW as a radar car.

Along with employment and social services, the Autobahn and the Volkswagen ranked among the successes that made the regime popular among the people.

A parade of Volkswagens, presented in 1938 at a propaganda event. Note the unusual shape of the front fender with the raised area over the headlight.

April/Mai 1939.

*6 Mann*

| | | |
|---|---|---|
| 26.4.39 | Modellschau Berlin(Pg.Meurer ca.8 Wochen) | 1 Wagen |
| 29.4.-2.5. | Deutsch-amerikan.Petrol.Ges.Hamburg, Neuer Jungfernstieg 21 | 1 Wagen |
| 1.-3.5. | Presse-und Filmfahrt Nürburgring Hotel Nürburg, Adenau | 3 Wagen |
| 5.-14.5. | Ostpreussenfahrt Königsberg z.V. Korpführer Hühnlein | 1 Wagen |
| ~~7.5.~~ | ~~Hamburger-Stadtparkrennen~~ | ~~2 Wagen~~ |
| 10.-14.5. | Breslauer Messe (Gauwagenwart Schlesien,Breslau 1 Kloster- str.8 ) | 1 Wagen |
| 13.-19.5. | Gau-und Kulturtagung in Stettin (Gauwagenwart Pommern,Stettin,Heiligen- geiststrasse 7 a) | 1 Wagen |
| 21.5. | Eifelrennen | 3 Wagen |
| 25.5. | Berlin, Ufafilm(10-14 Tage) | 2 Wagen Cabrio |

Juni 1939.

| | | |
|---|---|---|
| 1.-12.6. | Ostmarkschau in Passau,Nibelungenhalle Gauwagenwart Bayreuth,Friedrichstrasse 39 | 3 Wagen |
| 1.-24.6. | Deutschlandfahrt Pressewagen | 1 Wagen Cabrio |
| 8.-15.6. | Berlin, Ufa | 2 Wagen |
| 18.6. | Motorradrennen Nürnberg | 2 Wagen |

Juli 1939.

| | | |
|---|---|---|
| 10.7. | Berlin, Großaufnahmen für Ufa | 10 Wagen |

Stgt.-Zuffenhausen, 26.4.1939.                              Koh/Ra.

A Volkswagen at the Grossglockner in 1938. Wherever the new KdF-Wagen turned up, it attracted attention and curiosity.

# Gemeinschaftslager Volkswagenwerk

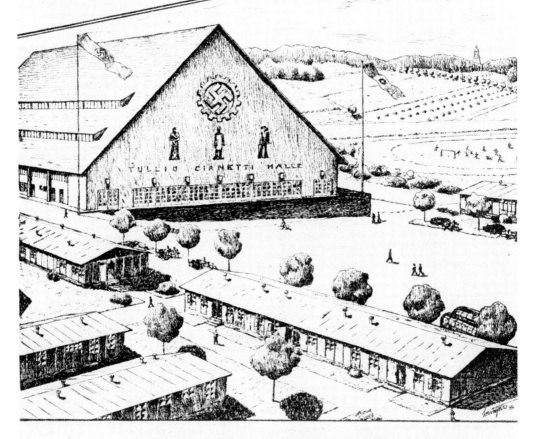

# Werkzeitschrift
## des Gemeinschaftslagers Volkswagenwerk

Jahrgang 1          Stadt des KdF.-Wagens, Februar 1939          Folge 1

The Cianetti Hall was built for organized spare-time and propaganda activities. It took its name from Tullio Cianetti, President of the Italian Fascist workers' organization. Along with Dr. Robert Ley, leader of the German Workers' Front, Cianetti laid the cornerstone for it on June 27, 1938.

A VW convertible (Porsche Type 60), photographed on the Autobahn near Stuttgart in 1941. The directional signals are mounted at an angle on the front window frames.

The convertible shown here had especially fine fittings: leather seats, radio, light-colored steering wheel and dashboard. The light-colored paint was an extra feature, for the uniform color of the VW was gray-blue-black. Another noteworthy detail is the external windshield-wiper rod.

An invalid car of 1939 (Porsche Type 67)

# Kübelwagen Before World War II

As of 1924, the Reichswehr leadership, in the process of rebuilding the army, began to find ways to get around the terms of the Treaty of Versailles, imposed by the victorious powers, and to resist the Entente sanctions. At the end of the crisis year of 1923, the economic and political conditions in Germany appeared to have stabilized, so that the prerequisites for an efficient future armament economy seemed to be at hand. The reorganization of the Reichswehr into a powerful Wehrmacht that could protect the German Reich from enemies was envisioned by the chief of army command, Generaloberst Hans von Seeckt, as including the full motorization of the remaining seven divisions as a mobile striking force, for the experiences of World War I had emphasized the importance of the automobile in front-line service.

In the early 1920s, the Reichswehr units had to be satisfied with production cars, for what with the tense financial situation, neither the military budget nor the manufacturers could possibly afford the development of special motor vehicles suited to military use. Because of the low selling price and the anticipated low maintenance costs, the army leadership favored the small car or that of the medium displacement class, so that even a midget like the BMW Dixi could hold its own in the army.

In the choice of vehicles to be obtained, of course, criteria were imposed that were based on the type of use. Thus front-drive cars were not taken into consideration at first because of the technology that was then still quite faulty. The military leadership thought well of rear drive and rugged rigid axles. As of about 1930, vehicles with swing-axle chassis were also included for testing purposes.

Only closed cars remained completely unchanged – except for their military camouflage paint. Naturally the open body style offered the decisive advantage for military action: they could be gotten into and out of – even jumped out of – most quickly. For protection against wind and rain, there were only a simple tent-canvas cover and rolled-up side curtains (instead of doors). The well-shaped bucket seats gave lateral support and protection against suddenly falling out sideways, and because of their appearance, they were soon given the name of "Kübelsitze" in soldier slang, which led to "Kübelsitzwagen" or simply "Kübelwagen." The term was retained for all subsequent open off-road passenger vehicles, even when they were no longer equipped with bucket seats, such as the Volkswagen Type 82 (which dispensed with bucket seats because it had solid doors) or the VW 181 (Bundeswehr).

In order to make personnel cars more useful for off-road use, several modifications were made. For example, the rear-axle ratio was increased, a locking differential installed and the suspension strengthened. To increase ground clearance, larger wheels were used and low-lying parts such as exhaust pipes and brake rods were moved. These measures were applied to the military versions of the Volkswagen as of 1940.

The design of the Kübelwagen resulted from cooperation between the Reichswehr and the German industry. Daimler-Benz, Horch and Wanderer built complete Kübelwagen; other firms delivered chassis that were completed by involved coach building firms.

The highly unfavorable numbers of models resulted from the fact that the commanders of the defensive districts could choose the contents of their motor parks freely, and thus local firms were usually given preference (for example, Stoewer in Stettin in District II). On the other hand, though, the Reich Defense Ministry wanted to give the German auto industry, badly damaged by inflation and economic crisis, a lift and involve as many firms as possible. Since the ranks were generally filled with production vehicles. which were now subject to regular model changes, the result was a great mixture of types.

Among the first Ku"belwagen models were the Adler Favorit, Hanomag 3/16 PS and the Wanderer W 11 (all built as of 1928-29). They were followed by other vehicles from a variety of manufacturers, divided into light or heavy weight classes. Among the light off-road PKW were the BMW 309 (4 cyl., 1934) and 315 (6 cyl., 1934), the Hanomag Types 3/16 PS, 4.20 PS (1930), 4/23 PS (1932) and, as of 1934 the Garant, Kurier and Rekord. And this group naturally included the military versions of the Volkswagen (Kübel, Schwimmwagen, VW Beetle) as of 1940-1942.

One class higher, that of the medium off-road PKW, included the Adler Standard 6, the Horch 8-30 (8 cyl.), the Mercedes Stuttgart 8/38 and 10/50, 260, 290, etc.

Most of the heavy off-road PKW were light trucks: Mercedes 1500 A, Steyr 1500 A.

The Army called for in the rearmament policy in effect since 1933, armed and motorized in very modern fashion, also set new standards in motor vehicles. The hard-hitting offensive Wehrmacht expected by Hitler had to be mobile, particularly on the battlefield. As the economy improved in the 1930s, the financial limits also disappeared.

In order to test production passenger cars for their military off-road capability, the Reichswehr took part, with open Kübelwagen and off-road sports cars, in the well-known trials and competitions sponsored by the German Automobile Club in the central mountains of Germany. The Black Forest high-altitude events, the three-day Harz Mountain run, and the off-road trials in Bavaria, Brandenburg and East Prussia were very popular.

In the off-road sporting events, which were taken over by the state as of 1933 and organized by the "Nationalsozialistischer Kraftfahrkorps" (NSKK), the vehicles were often tested for utility, load carrying and ruggedness in winter conditions. Almost all the vehicles were open production cars, convertibles or roadsters, not even true sports cars, powered as they were by ordinary motors, but just simple everyday cars with open, sporting bodywork, and without all-wheel drive, locking differentials, slow or off-road gears. Their achievements off the road, in trackless fields, swamps and mud, and on steep slopes, were modest by today's standards. Yet these off-road events for the purpose of testing the materials under extreme conditions were important for the manufacturers, which had no test facilities of their own yet. And the state naturally took an interest in the sense of paramilitary driver training. NSKK Leader Konrad Hühnlein explained: "The driving sport has become a people's sport in the service of the nation."

Few private drivers took part in these events; the great majority of the participants were recruited from the factory teams, the Reichswehr or Wehrmacht (as of 1935), the party organizations or the German Automobile Club.

Very good records were achieved in these events by: the Hanomag Rekord (1.5 liters, 4 cylinders, ohc, 35 HP, 1933-39) and Sturm (2.3 liters, 6 cylinders, ohc, 57 HP, 1934-39), the Wanderer W 40 (2 liters, 6 cylinders, ohc, 40 HP), the DKW Reichsklasse (0.6 liter, 2 cylinders, two-stroke, 18 HP, 1935-39) and Meisterklasse (0.7 liter, 2 cylinders, two-stroke, 20 HP, 1935-39), the Opel Super 6 (2.5 liters, 6 cylinders, 55 HP; the same motor as in the "Kapitän" after the war). Also of note was the Adler Triumph (1.5 and 1.7 liters, 4 cylinders, side valves, 30, 38 and 45 HP), which even existed with a remarkably un-angular special chassis. On the other hand, the rear-engine Mercedes 130 Kübel was a disappointment, though it much resembled the later VW Kübelwagen which was so admired.

To deal with the irrational multiplicity of models, the concept of a uniform type was advocated and found lively support when the Wehrmacht was built up as of 1933. The chassis of the uniform personnel cars were classified, corresponding to the previous division, as light, medium and heavy off-road cars. Various firms were given contracts for the development of the uniform cars according to specifications of the Army Weapons Office (including all-wheel drive and steering). The uniform types were supposed to afford economical mass production, standardization of aggregates and easy inter-changeability of parts. In view of the rapidly growing numbers of military vehicles, storage, repair and supply in case of war were to be simplified radically.

At first the Stoewer Works in Stettin received a contract to produce a light uniform off-road car. At the 1936 International Automobile Show the finished prototype was displayed to the public. But since Stoewer did not have sufficient production capacity, BMW and Hanomag (in Hannover) were also chosen to produce further series in 1937. These light uniform personnel cars were not as uniform as the name suggests. Depending on who made them, they had different motors with different numbers of cylinders (4 or 6), different displacements (1.8 or 2 liters, 42 or 50 HP), mechanical or hydraulic brake systems, two- or four-wheel steering, two- or four-wheel drive, etc. The exchanging of individual aggregates was thus possible only with great difficulty.

Unfortunately, experience gained by using the light uniform PKW brought bitter disappointment to the hopes embodied in it. The vehicle was much too expensive to build, too heavy off the road, to complicated and prone to require repairs. As a result, production was cut down as of 1940 and finally halted altogether. It was replaced with the Mercedes 170 V with Kübel body, and finally by the VW Kübelwagen, which was built in great numbers as of 1940 and made available to the troops. Both vehicles lacked all-wheel drive, but were extremely rugged and reliable. Without a doubt, the Volkswagen was superior to the Mercedes as an off-road car. The 170 VK was too heavy and had too little ground clearance. On the other hand, the VW Kübel could utilize its light weight, greater clearance and well-known VW advantages: rear drive plus the weight of the motor, air-cooling and oil cooler (favorable in extreme climates, as in the African and Russian theaters of war).

A very superficial comparison shows that the concept of the VW Kübelwagen was right:

| light uniform | PKW | MB 170 VK | VW Kübel |
|---|---|---|---|
| Weight (kilograms) | 1775 | 1235 | 725 |
| Ground clearance (mm) | 235 | 200 | 290 |
| Fuel consumption (L) | 17-25 | 13 | 8 |

Werner Oswald writes on the subject: "Nobody before Porsche had gotten the idea that it could be practical to make off-road vehicles very light and simple instead of massive and complicated. He was also right to consider a small, air-cooled one-liter motor to be fully sufficient."

Hitler himself spoke in favor of a simple design at that time. On April 9, 1942 he said: "For military reasons, a limitation of the German auto production to ten or twelve types after the war would be appropriate, in order to direct the genius of our inventors toward a far-reaching simplification of motors . . . The most important factor, though, would be the creation of a uniform motor that could be installed in field kitchens as well as ambulances, and also in reconnaissance vehicles, tractors and towing vehicles for heavy infantry guns. The 28 HP motor of the Volkswagen would be quite sufficient for these military purposes. This very war is the best evidence that nothing can be won in war at top speed. Therefore we absolutely must get away from all the high-speed automobiles. The uniform motor to be striven for . . . would have to be easily changeable, since – as this war is teaching us – the supplying of spare parts causes more trouble than taking an intact motor out of a vehicle with a damaged chassis." (quoted from Henry Picker & Heinrich Hoffmann, Hitlers Tischgespräche)

# Personnel Cars and Motorcycles of the Wehrmacht

Since the German Wehrmacht did not possess sufficient numbers of a useful light off-road car (lei. Pkw) when the war began, the various army units were originally assigned many vehicles requisitioned from private owners.

The big, heavy cars made by Audi, Horch, Mercedes and Maybach do not need to be considered here, for they do not belong in the same class as our Volkswagen and were reserved for high-ranking officers, commanders or staffs. On the other hand, the smaller civilian vehicles, roughly in the displacement class between 1.3 and 2.5 liters, could be found in military service anywhere. These production sedans, convertibles or cabrio-sedans, which were simply painted in dull military colors and marked with tactical symbols, certainly had not been developed for military service and thus were generally useful only within limits, such as in back-line areas, in delivery service, at bases back home or among the occupation forces.

The various types of Opel performed well, especially the Olympia and the Super 6 with their rugged chassis and reliably running motors. The Olympia convertible was frequently used to lead a column. Since Opel had been the most prevalent make of car in Germany before the war, and since many Opels had also been exported – to Holland, Belgium and Denmark, among others – many requisitioned Opels were to be found in the Wehrmacht.

Most of the civilian Ford cars were also requisitioned for war service, especially the Eifel and V 8 types.

The larger V 8 was often prepared and rebuilt for heavy work on account of its massive construction: as a towing vehicle or limber, radio car or ambulance, with box body or welded-on equipment containers.

The Mercedes 170 V was used in large numbers as a Kübelwagen (170 VK). From 1938 to 1942, 19,000 of them were built. Thus it attained second place among the most often-built Kübelwagen, second only to the VW Kübel. But the 170 sedan and 170 convertibles built for civilian use were also requisitioned, as were all other similar open or closed German cars, such as Adler, BMW, Horch, Steyr, Stoewer and Wanderer.

DKW – a popular and widespread make in Germany before the war –was largely excused from war service. The low-powered two-cylinder F 5, F 7 and F 8 with their wooden bodies covered with imitation leather were simply not suitable. There was a bucket-seat version of the "Sonderklasse", but DKW, what with its two-stroke concept, was out of place from the start.

In 1939 the German makes were joined by the Czech products, Skoda and Tatra, from the newly created "Protectorate" of Bohemia and Moravia. During the war, many foreign cars made in Britain or France also fell into German hands. Goodly numbers of cars made by Austin, Morris, Wolseley, Citroen, Peugeot and Renault were used by the German military forces. Many of them, such as the renowned Citroen 11 CV, came to grief in the mud of Russia. The French were quite strongly represented, as the French automobile factories were included in German war production after the occupation of France.

The main disadvantage of the requisitioned cars resulted from their low ground clearance. In addition, the springs, shock absorbers, steering, etc. were generally much too weak to stand up to extreme conditions.

Despite all efforts, a chronic shortage of vehicles existed in the German Reich during the war – even when the VW Kübel reached the troops in great numbers as the universal light military vehicle. A comparison between the German and American production figures clearly shows the weakness of German motorization: while some 52,000 Kübel were produced and put into service in the German Reich, 650,000 Jeeps were built in the USA. This sad story scarcely improves when the approximately 15,000 VW Schwimmwagen and the 14,000 light uniform PKW by Stoewer, BMW and Hanomag are added, especially as the last soon dropped out of use because of their frequent need of repairs.

The Volkswagen Kübel, which was used more and more often as a light off-road car from 1940-1941 on, was really a successful design: light, rugged, extremely reliable, economical to maintain and cheap to produce. Along with its close relative the Schwimmwagen, it was also to replace the majority of the motorcycles or horse-drawn wagons that often had to give up the struggle quickly when used off the road. Early in January 1943 Hitler gave instructions that production of the VW Kübelwagen was to increase at the cost of motorcycles with sidecars as soon as magnesium could be used in the VW. The Volkswagen, he asserted, was superior because of the possibility of its towing a trailer. It was therefore the future solution, since it had more fighting power, protected its driver from dust, coldness and wind, and was considerably less costly to maintain.

Thus the future of the motorcycle in military use looked hopeless at the time. Motorcycles with sidecars had already been valued in World War I as motorized machine-gun positions and for fast courier service. At that time the motorcycle, compared to the heavy and ponderous cars of the time, had shown itself to be useful on account of its lightness, quickness and mobility. Its economy and low production cost were additional advantages. As a result, when the Reichswehr was reorganized as of 1927, its range of use in reconnaissance, communication and supply units and in tactical service was expanded considerably. Cycles with armed soldiers were soon organized into their own cycle companies as very fast-moving attack units.

When the Wehrmacht was organized in 1935, the motorcycle riflemen became a service arm of their own. In the western campaign, the cycle units proved themselves well. As the war spread into the Balkans, to Africa and the Soviet Union, the limits of its utility soon became apparent. On the extensive road network of western Europe and in the cultivated rural areas there, the cycle soldiers could go into action quickly. The roadless areas in the East made the highest demands on them. The heavy vehicles got stuck in the Russian mud all too often. Moving in columns on the rutted and dusty roads, across the fields or through the mountains in the Balkan countries, the cycles were often more burdened than they could stand.

To take the place of the impractical motorcycles, more and more of the two rugged, off-road capable Volkswagens were delivered to the troops from 1941 on. They were also less costly (the price of a VW Kübel was 2945 RM, half as much as a Zündapp KS 750 with driven sidecar). Many Kübel- and Schwimmwagen were thus found, as the pictures in this book will show, with shock troops and reconnaissance units. The VW Schwimmwagen with its all-wheel drive and its short, compact and rounded body was, in fact, predestined for its frequent designation as "motorcycle rifle car."

# The Volkswagen as a Military Vehicle
## The Kübelwagen

In the "Exposé concerning the construction of a German People's Car", which was compiled by Porsche in 1934 and presented to the Reich Transport Ministry, the parameters for the technical conception of the Volkswagen had been included: air-cooling, rear engine, swing axle, rear-wheel drive and torsion-bar suspension were envisioned. The traditional frame construction with the body placed and screwed onto it allowed various bodies, a prerequisite for the design of an open military version.

In 1938 the preliminary work began on the military utility of the VW, which culminated in the well-known Kübelwagen and, later, the Schwimmwagen.

According to instructions from the Army Weapons Office, the following guidelines were established for the military adaptation of the VW: open body, 950 kilograms gross weight (550 kg vehicle weight, 400 kg for three men and one machine gun).

After the bad experiences with the uniform Pkw, great emphasis was placed on lightness, low-cost modification of the VW sedan into a military vehicle, and low production cost.

On November 3, 1938 the first prototype of the VW Kübelwagen was finished, and a few days later it was subjected to exhaustive tests at the troop training camp near Münsingen. In 1939 there appeared the next stage of development, the angular Type 62, which bore much similarity to the finished product. The off-road capability of this vehicle, though, did not satisfy the Army High Command. Porsche undertook further modifications: among others, increasing the ground clearance, installing reduction gears on the rear half-axle to increase the torque. In addition, the front of the car was raised.

The first examples of the finished Type 82 appeared in December 1939. At the same time, work began on the four-wheel-drive versions of the Kübelwagen (Type 86/87). Two prototypes were made; they were tested in February 1940 (on the Kummersdorf-St. Johann in Tirol road, sometimes using snow slides. In March and April, eleven Type 82 and two Type 86 cars were summoned for comparison tests (column and off-road driving with tactical use). Comparison tests in the spring of 1940 showed clearly that the newly-developed Volkswagens were superior to the BMW and Zündapp sidecar motorcycles in rough country. This led to the decision to introduce the VW in place of the motorcycles as "motorcycle rifle wagons."

Series production of the Kübelwagen began in the spring of 1940; in April, 25 vehicles were built in Stuttgart, and from May on, production took place at the VW factory: 100 in May, 200 in June, 275 in July. The 1000th Kübel was finished on December 20.

A great constructive advantage of the Kübelwagen was its lightness, which meant that four-wheel drive could be done away with once and for all. In times of need, two or three men could lift the vehicle.

The advantage of the air-cooled motor at that time was that it was insensitive to extreme climate. Weather in boiling heat in Africa or icy cold in the vastness of Russia, the VW motor kept running. And for a long time this was also one reason for the Beetle's enormous export success. The simple construction was also esteemed by the soldiers in the war, as all components were easy to get at. The motor could be lifted out of the rear end after a few twists when the body bulkhead was unscrewed. And the VW soon acquired a good reputation for its extraordinary ruggedness and reliability, a prerequisite for the steadily ascending career of the Volkswagen after the war. In addition, the Kübelwagen developed strong traction thanks to its reduction gears and thus was a capable off-road vehicle, what with its high ground clearance.

This convincing concept, now that it had been found, was to be used in as many ways as possible. A number of variations were developed from the normal version – the four-seat personnel car: radio car, barrel carrier, wounded transporter, halftrack, dummy tank, railcar, siren car, range-finding and intelligence car.

In addition, there were a whole series of added or built-in aggregates that were mounted on the rear of the vehicle and powered by the motor, such as a pump or a starter gear.

According to VW factory data, the following numbers were produced:

| | |
|---|---|
| Kübelwagen, four-seat personnel car | 37,320 |
| Kübelwagen, intelligence car | 7,545 |
| Kübelwagen, radio car | 3,326 |
| Kübelwagen, repair-shop car | 273 |

Plus individual specimens for testing purposes.

# The Schwimmwagen

The work of developing an amphibious off-road car went on at Porsche KG since July 1940.

In the 1930s, Hanns Trippel had made a name for himself with amphibious projects. Trippel worked independently in Darmstadt since 1932 and had attracted the attention of the Third Reich leadership with his noteworthy designs. He was given support and was able to open his own company, with 250 employees, in Homburg on the Saar. From then on, Trippel was working for the Wehrmacht. He became known throughout Europe when he crossed the Gulf of Naples to Capri in an amphibian he had built. Larger capacities were made available to him in 1940, when he was able to expand his production into the former Bugatti factory in Molsheim, Alsace. There, on January 15, 1941, under the support of the "Bank of German Air Travel", which was subordinate to Hermann Goering's Air Ministry, the Trippel Werke GmbH was founded. About a thousand Trippel SG 6 amphibians, driven by Opel Kapitän motors, were built by 1944.

The military interest in amphibian cars and the great expectations inspired by the new Volkswagen naturally led to the development of an amphibian based on the VW concept for the Wehrmacht. A modern box principle was an essential part of the plan. The Porsche design bureau was then given subsequent work. On July 8, the Army Weapons Office issued a contract for three amphibians (Type 128). The first test vehicle was finished on September 21. On November 1, the three prototypes were turned over, and on November 5-6 the VW/Porsche Type 128 ("long amphibian") was tested for the first time. The further development was hastened in the spring of 1941. Several long test drives were undertaken at that time, including those in Tyrol, the Black Forest and Lake Constance areas, in the Balkans and in Libya.

Since the large hull of the VW 128 had shown itself to be too unstable in all of these tests and also limited its off-road capability, a car with a shorter wheelbase and smaller hull (Type 166) was developed in August 1941; on the basis of tests, the results of which were positive, it replaced the Type 128 and went into production at the VW works in the summer of 1942. From the end of 1942 on, the VW 166 was supplied to the troops in large numbers (particularly to Waffen-SS units). The bodies were not built by VW, but by Ambi Budd in Berlin, a branch of the American firm of the same name.

The Schwimmwagen was fitted with wide tires of various sizes (200-12 or 200-16). But as the pictures in this book show, many of them ran, for reasons of practicality and for lack of rubber, on normal VW tires (size 5.25-16). The Schwimmwagen was also fitted with a more powerful motor (1131 cc, 24.5 HP) from the start. As of March 1943 this motor was used in all Volkswagens.

By the end of 1944, 14,276 Schwimmwagen had been finished in Wolfsburg; then production had to be halted because of heavy bombing of the factory. In the uneasy war situation, the considerable outlay of materials and manpower for the complicated vehicle was no longer possible. Only the simple Kübelwagen continued to be produced until the spring of 1945.

# The VW Beetle

Production of the KdF-Wagen was cut back when the war began, but not halted altogether. From 1938 to 1940, 54 sedans and six convertibles were built, from 1942 to 1944 another 650 sedans and 13 convertible Beetles.

In addition, the body of the KdF-Wagen was combined with the chassis of the Kübelwagen. The VW sedan on the Kübel chassis can be spotted immediately, even by the layman, on account of its high ground clearance. With the reduction gears and auxiliary shafts of its rear half-axles, the off-road Beetle had a lot of motive power in its lower gears and it rose up abruptly on its hind wheels during steady driving in first or second gear. In regard to its off-road capability, this Beetle had all the features of the Kübelwagen whose lower components it took over. The closed Beetle body had the additional advantage of offering protection against cold, rain, wind and dust. But otherwise the narrow Beetle body had nothing but disadvantages in war service. For shock troops who had to jump out quickly or keep watch, as a reconnaissance or rifle car, the off-road sedan was scarcely suitable. And as we all know, a Beetle is also problematic when it comes to stowing luggage.

The off-road Beetle was designated Type 92 or, as of April 1943, Type 82 E. Production continued, with small numbers built, from October 1942 to 1944. The total number remained small, at 564 (plus two convertibles). But at least two cars were built in 1941. These cars went to the Colonial Political Office of the Reich Foreign Ministry, a non-military agency. Therefore these cars, although military vehicles, had gloss paint and chromed parts. The two Volkswagens were sent with a convoy to Afghanistan; their route went from Berlin via Bohemia, Hungary, Rumania, Bulgaria, Turkey and Iran to Kabul (May 27 to December 8, 1941). Between Istanbul and Trapezunt they went by ship on the Black Sea. The German embassy in Kabul, as an outpost of German power in the Orient in World War II, took on a certain importance in the support of revolutionary Arabic nationalists in their fight against British colonial power. In the Colonial Political Office, it was intended at that time to supply the civilian governmental structure in the future with off-road Volkswagens of Types 82, 82 E, 87 and 166 equipped for the tropics.

Most of the off-road Beetles were turned over to various SS units (Type 92 SS) and were equipped more for demonstration purposes in photographs than for combat use with hand-operated guns installed (MP 38-40).

On the basis of the VW 82 E, two delivery vans were also built: one vehicle with a pickup body (Type 825) and one with a box body, the so-called tropic wagon (Type 81). For these utilitarian vehicles, the Kübel chassis with its reduction gears for better low-end torque was very useful.

The most technically interesting Beetle of all is the four-wheel-drive sedan – a combination of the KdF body and the 4wd Kübelwagen chassis. The four-wheel-drive Type 87/92 SS, like all other military variations, naturally has an additional transmission and a production locking differential (at both ends in the Type 86/87). Unlike the off-road Beetle 92/82 E, the Type 87/92 SS has special axle shanks to take the driveshafts. In addition, there is an added off-road gear. A second shift lever engages the reduction gears and the front-wheel drive. For reasons of space, the hand-brake lever was moved forward and to the side. The 4wd Beetle had huge off-road wheels, and thus also widened fenders and running boards, plus a large opening roof hatch (cabrio-limousine).

How many four-wheel-drive Beetles were actually built cannot be determined precisely. According to information from the VW factory, there were 564 of them, most of which were delivered to the Afrika-Korps. More recent studies have indicated that this number is not definite, since all 4wd vehicles are basically included in the Type 87 designation – including those with the Kübel body. It is possible that only three 4wd Beetles were built: two in 1941, which were used for testing in the Balkans, and one further model in Stuttgart in 1943; it was photographed in detail there, as will be seen in this book. The rest of the Type 87 Volkswagens were 4wd Kübelwagen.

On the subject of types, we must add that the Type 87 designation is a collective concept, and that additional digits specify the type of vehicle:

Type 87        Chassis with four-wheel drive
Type 87 0      Kübelwagen body (four-seat)
Type 87 1      Kübelwagen body (three-seat)
Type 87 7      Closed sedan body (command car)

For the four-wheel-drive Beetle there were three type designations: 877, 92 SS and 98. Whether three different versions were actually built, though, remains questionable. The Type 92 SS was built only with the Kübelwagen chassis, thus without four-wheel drive. Of the Type 98 (cabrio-limousine with 4wd), apparently only the one example was built by Porsche in Stuttgart. Subsequent rebuildings (perhaps built at the factory) can scarcely be proved to exist, since they are not listed in the records at Wolfsburg. Once in a while a 4wd chassis may have been fitted with a Beetle body in place of the Kübel body after the war, or a 4wd Beetle built out of Schwimmwagen components. But such vehicles cannot be regarded as original types.

# Types and Development Numbers

| | |
|---|---|
| Type 60 | German Volkswagen |
| | L Limousine (sedan) |
| | CL Cabrio-limousine (open-roof sedan) |
| | Cabrio (open convertible) |
| | LO Lieferwagen (open pickup truck) |
| Type 61 | Reduced-size study |
| Type 62 | Volkswagen for off-road use (Kübelwagen prototype) |
| Type 64 | Berlin-Rome Car (VW record car) |
| Type 65 | Special equipment for driving schools |
| Type 66 | VW Type 60 with right-hand drive |
| Type 67 | VW Type 60 as invalid car |
| Type 68 | VW Type 60 as delivery van |
| Type 81 | VW box van |
| Type 82 | Volkswagen for off-road use (production Kübelwagen) |
| | 0 four-seat (normal version) |
| | 1 three-seat |
| | 2 siren car |
| | 3 dummy tank or scout car for training use |
| | 5 pickup truck with sedan body |
| | 6 box van with sedan body (tropical car) |
| | 7 three-seat command car |
| | 8 open body (made of wood) |
| | E Kübel chassis with sedan body (off-road Beetle) |
| Type 86 | Kübelwagen with four-wheel drive (prototype) |
| Type 87 | Four-wheel-drive chassis (based on Type 82) |
| | O four-seat Kübelwagen body |
| | 1 three-seat Kübelwagen body |
| | 7 sedan body (command car) |
| Type 88 | Delivery van, Model B |
| Type 89 | automatic transmission (experiment) |
| Type 92 | Type 82 chassis with sedan (Beetle) body |
| | SS with weapons, with/without four-wheel drive |
| | LO open pickup truck |
| | open body, KdF cabrio (convertible) |
| Type 98 | Cabrio-limousine (open-roof) with four-wheel drive |
| Type 106 | Experimental transmission |
| Type 107 | Turbocharger |
| Type 115 | Supercharged motor |
| Type 120 | Stationary motor for Reich Air Ministry |
| Type 121 | Stationary motor for Army Weapons Office (magneto) |
| Type 122 | Stationary motor for Reich Postal System |
| Type 126 | fully synchronized gearbox |
| Type 127 | pusher motor (experimental) |
| Type 128 | Schwimmwagen, first version |
| Type 129 | Schwimmwagen, special version |
| Type 138 | Schwimmwagen, Type B |
| Type 155 | Type 82 with tire-chain equipment |
| Type 157 | railcar equipment for VW 82/87 |
| Type 160 | VW Limousine, self-supporting body |
| Type 162 | Off-road car with self-supporting body |
| Type 164 | 6-wheel off-road car with two motors |
| Type 166 | Schwimmwagen, improved production version |
| Type 177 | 5-speed transmission for off-road VW |
| Type 179 | VW with fuel injection |
| Type 182 | Off-road car with uniform body (2-wheel drive) |
| Type 187 | Off-road car with uniform body (4-wheel drive) |

| | |
|---|---|
| Type 198 | Starter drive |
| Type 230 | VW with generator power |
| Type 231 | VW with acetylene power |
| Type 235 | VW with electric power |
| Type 239 | VW with wood-gas generator |
| Type 240 | VW with bottle-gas power |
| Type 247 | VW aircraft motor |
| Type 276 | VW Type 82 with towing hook |
| Type 278 | Synchronized gearbox |
| Type 283 | Type 82 with generator power |
| Type 287 | Command car body (improved 4wd), KdF body |
| Type 296 | Intermediate gears for VW motor |
| Type 307 | Heavy-duty carburetor |
| Type 309 | Diesel motor (experiment) |
| Type 330 | VW sedan with wood-gas mixer |
| Type 331 | VW with native fuel system |
| Type 332 | VW with anthracite coal system |

# Modifications to the VW Kübelwagen

(Source: VW factory spare part lists for Type 82, 3/43, 5/44)

Chassis numbers beginning with

| | |
|---|---|
| 1 501 | Clutch with two pressure springs (previously one) |
| 4 402 | Ignition lock with uniform key |
| 5 000 | Long rear fender with reinforcement |
| 6 803 | Gear housing on longitudinal member, with 5 screws (previously 3) |
| 8 500 | Plug-in jack with hexagonal key, longitudinal member with hole for jack (previously scissor jack) |
| 9 001 | Wide cover panel for underside of motor |
| 9 501 | Exhaust to side of motor (previously as on VW sedan), new: heating |
| 11 280 | Rear-wheel drive housing with new type of screws |
| 14 001 | Larger fuel filler |
| 15 371 | Cross tubes between front and rear towing hooks, socket for starter no longer screwed to motor cover panel, but as footrest in middle of rear crossbar, rear cover panel screwed on |
| 15 518 | Starting fuel container |
| 15 656 | No turn signals |
| 17 001 | No starter |
| 25 001 | Small dashboard from Schwimmwagen used, small speedometer (VW sedan dash board previously used) |
| 29 001 | Emblem on left of motor hood, hood louvers thus shortened (previously with emblem projecting over side) |

Chassis numbers beginning with

| | |
|---|---|
| 20 292 | Greater displacement and power: 1131 cc, 24.5 HP (previously 985 cc, 23.5 HP) |
| 32 624 | Centrifugal air filter (previously oil-bath type) |

# Modifications to the VW Beetle

Production changes in the VW sedan are hard to identify, since the details in the small series often changed from one vehicle to the next.

Several typical identifying marks of the 1938-1940 pre-production cars are: motor cooling vents under the rear window with 48 louvers, motor and trunk hoods with sharp upper edges, hood braces to lower end with support rods (no return spring). The noticeable, somewhat bulging roof shape inside by the rear window is different from that of the later types. The KdF-VW original had chromed bumpers with rounded convex (to the inside) horns, steering wheel with thick spokes, glove compartment with door, and no heater. Other features: license-plate lights with brake light above, hubcaps without emblem, right dashboard attachment with switch scheme, turning knobs.

Series production of the KdF-Wagen ran from July 11, 1941 to August 17, 1944 (production then halted because of war conditions).

Changes to the body: Front and rear hoods rounded to the side at upper ends, 42 cooling louvers, in interior: five slits below rear window (previously two). Further details: flat hubcaps with VW emblem and geared ring, bumper horns pointed and concave (curved outward), no glove compartment door, new license-plate lights with brake light below.

Further changes during course of production:

From 1942 on: starting crank aperture in rear bumper.

March 1943: Motor with 1131 cc, 24.5 HP (previously 985 cc, 23.5 HP).

1943: Bigger fuel tank, front end of car modified to hold it, painted bumpers, more ways to save material: hubcaps, bumper horns, rear-view mirror, turn signals, starter eliminated, simple seats as in Kübelwagen, combination taillight on left fender (no license-plate light on motor hood), steering wheel with thin spokes.

# VOLKSWAGENWERK

Gesellschaft mit beschränkter Haftung, Sitz Berlin

ZENTRALE BERLIN

BERLIN W15 · KNESEBECKSTRASSE 48/49 · FERNRUF: 91 91 91

Einschreiben
An die
Dr. ing. h.c.F- Porsche K.-G.
z.Hd. d.Herrn Baron v. Malberg
oder Vertreter im Amt
Stuttgart-Zuffenhausen
Spitalwaldstrasse 2

| Ihre Zeichen | Ihre Nachricht vom | Unsere Zeichen | Datum |
|---|---|---|---|
| | | X/Dr.St./Hr. | 7.11.1939 |

Sehr geehrter Herr Baron von Malberg!

Unter Bezugnahme auf die am Donnerstag den 2.d.Mts. mit
Ihnen gehabte Unterredung, übermitteln wir Ihnen in der
Anlage die Abschrift unseres Angebotes an das Oberkommando
des Heeres, sowie die nach Ihren Angaben festgelegte Vorka
kulation für die Kriegsaufträge Wa Prüf 6/Ia 106-0050/39
und Wa Prüf 6/Ib 106-0948/39 zur gefl. Kenntnisnahme und s
zen hierbei voraus, dass Sie uns später bei der Ermittelun
der nachzuweisenden Kosten behilflich sein werden.

Aus steuertechnischen Gründen bitten wir, die Karosserie-
beschaffung beim Ambi-Budd-Presswerk namens und im Auftrage
des Volkswagenwerkes vorzunehmen, damit diese Rechnungen,
wenn wir sie als Nachweis der Selbstkosten etwa dem Oberkommando des Heeres vorlegen müssen, auf das Volkswagenwer
lauten.
Hierdurch ist eine verhältnismässig bedeutende Ersparnis
an Umsatzsteuer möglich.

Heil Hitler!
Volkswagenwerk
G.m.b.H. i.V.

Anlagen: 3 Blaupausen

33

Attachment points in the front storage space (with attached MG 34)

1. Lock (for tripod),          2. Protective sheath for MG,          3. Shooting rest

Attachment points over the front seats and on the rear side doors

1. Belt holder 34,                                3. MG mount,
2. Extension of upper gun holder,                4. Belt holder 34.

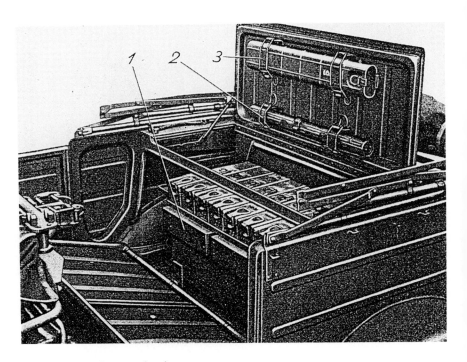

Attachment points in rear storage space

1. Rach for 14 bullet cases
(with cases in it),

2. Mount for barrel shield 34,
3. Mount for barrel holder 34.

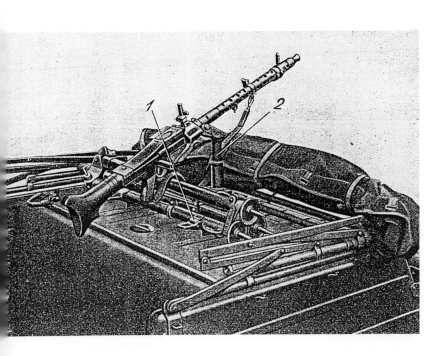

Attachment points on the rear storage space.

1. Lock for tripod,    2. MG holder.

Kübelwagen with snow slider.

Snow slider attached to front wheel

Driving tests with halftracks and snow sliders. The vehicles have civilian registrations from Stuttgart.

Test cars for dummy tanks.

Rear entrance hatch above the engine cover.

A look through the open hatch into the interior, showing the dashboard, driver's and gunner's seats.

Dummy tank, seen from interior.

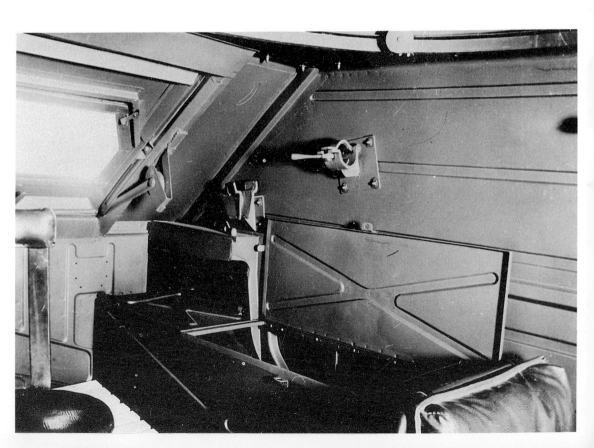

Front of the dummy tank

A Kübelwagen marked "Volkswagen Works Customer Service" crosses a wooden bridge.

Note the "Wolfsburg" sign on the building (named after the local castle). Until May 1945 the city was called "Stadt des KdF-Wagens."

A bracket holds the discs carried on the front hood during road and off-road trips. It is sturdier than the hood and prevents damage.

Volkswagen railcar.

VW/Porsche Type 155, snow vehicle, Version IV, with trailer hitch, 1942.

Track drive and exhaust system.

Chassis with halftracks.

Test rig for braking of one track.

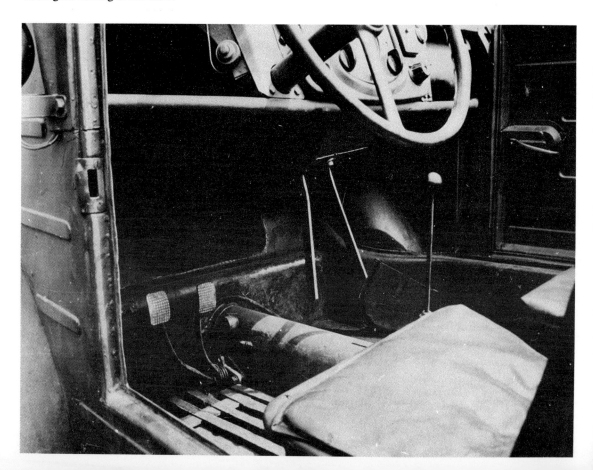

Three-seat Kübelwagen, prepared for use as a radio car.

Kübelwagen for transport of wounded, with racks to hold two stretchers, on above the other.

**Oberkommando des Heeres**
(Befehlshaber des Ersatzheeres)

76 b 1010 Wa Prüf 6 (Gr.I)
Bb.Nr. 4870/40 g.

(Bitte in der Antwort vorstehendes Geschäftszeichen, das Datum und kurzen Inhalt anzugeben)

Berlin W 35, den *18.* Juni 1940
Tirpitzufer 72-76
Fernsprecher: Ortsverkehr 21 00 12
Fernverkehr 21 00 16

Einschreiben

Geheim.

1. Dies ist ein Staatsgeheimnis ...
§ 88 ...

2. Weitergabe nur verschlossen, bei ...
"Einschreiben" ...

3. Aufbewahrung ... Empfängers
nur ...

Firma
Dr.Jng.h.c.F. P o r s c h e  K.-G.
Stuttgart - Zuffenhausen,
Spitalwaldstraße 2

Betr. Typ 128

Das Oberkommando des Heeres (Ch H Rüst u.B d E)
Wa Prüf 6 bittet zu überprüfen, ob es möglich ist, auf
der Basis des vierradangetriebenen Volkswagens einen
Gelände-Schwimm-Pkw. zu entwickeln. Das Fahrzeug soll
in erster Linie für Zwecke der Pioniere usw. eingesetzt
werden und wird von dieser Waffe vordringlich gefordert.

Als Anhaltspunkte können vorerst gegeben werden:
voll geländegängiger Pkw., Höchstgeschwindigkeit 80 km,
Steigfähigkeit wie vierradangetriebener Volkswagen, An-
trieb im Wasser mit Schraube, Geschwindigkeit im Wasser
mindestens 10 km, Steuerung im Wasser durch die Rad-
scheiben der gelenkten Vorderräder, mindestens Tragfähig-
keit im Wasser wie auf dem Lande. Auf Einstiegtüren usw.
kann verzichtet werden. Übergang von Land- zur Wasserfahrt
ohne Verlassen des Fahrzeuges.

Oberkommando des Heeres (Ch H Rüst u.B d E) Wa Prüf
wäre dankbar, wenn die Dr.Porsche K.-G. baldigst Stellung-
nahme zu dem Entwicklungsvorgang übermitteln könnte. Das
Vorhaben muß vorerst geheim gehalten werden.

Jm Auftrage

*[Unterschrift]*

Porsche

Technischer Schriftwechsel

| Abteilung | Tag | | | | |
|-----------|-----|--|--|--|--|
| Technisches Büro | | | | | |
| Porsche jun. | | | | | |

47

# VOLKSWAGENWERK

### Gesellschaft mit beschränkter Haftung, Sitz Berlin

STADT DES KDF-WAGENS

Firma

**Einschreiben**

Dr. Ing. h.c. F.Porsche K.-G.

Stuttgart-Zuffenhausen
Spitalwaldstrasse 2

Dr.ing.h.c.F. ... K.-G.
Stuttgart-Zuffenhausen ... Spitalwaldstr.2

140639 * -9 DEZ 1940

Technischer Schriftwechsel
Erledigt am 19...

| Ihre Zeichen | Ihre Nachricht vom | Unsere Zeichen | Datum |
|---|---|---|---|
| | | KA Rö/Ma- | 5.12.1940 |

Betr.: Unser Projekt 1o37/3.

Das Oberkommando des Heeres (Heereswaffenamt, Prüfwesen 6)
beabsichtigt, uns unter der Nr. Wa Prüf 6 )Ia) 006-02o2/4o
einen Kriegsauftrag zur Durchführung nachstehender Leistung
zu vergeben:

Bau eines Schwimm - Pkw. Typ 128

Zu berücksichtigen sind die bisherigen Ergebnisse der Werks-
erprobung und der Versuchsfahrt des OKH mit den 3 Fahrzeugen
aus Auftrag Wa Prüf 6/Ia 006-o111/4o.

Wir erteilen Ihnen hiermit den Auftrag zur Durchführung der
oben angegebenen Leistung. Gleichzeitig legen wir Ihnen For-
mulare zur Abgabe eines Festpreisangebotes bei und zwar

Angebotsformular und
Kalkulationsformular

in je 3-facher Ausfertigung.

Ist die Abgabe eines Festpreisangebotes in kurzer Zeit nicht
möglich, dann sind im Kalkulationsblatt nur die Stunden- und
Zuschlagsätze anzubieten, die bei der Abrechnung zur Anwen-
dung kommen sollen. Für Instandsetzungen können auch Stunden-
sätze angeboten werden, die alle Zuschläge enthalten. Für
Ersatzteile, die nach dem Umfang noch nicht feststehen, ist
anzugeben, dass spätere Berechnung zu Listenpreisen abzüglich
des festgelegten Rabattes erfolgt. Bei Konstruktionsaufträgen
sind Konstrukteur- und Zeichnerstunden anzubieten, die alle
Zuschläge enthalten. Am Schluss von Angeboten zu Selbstkosten

Water test of a prototype Schwimmwagen.

Schwimmwagen proto-
type (Kübelwagen in need
of repair in the back-
ground).

Schwimmwagen Type 128 (long version)

Dr. Ing. h.c.F. **Porsche** K.-G.

G e d ä c h t n i s p r o t o k o l l .

- - - - - - - - - - - - - - - - - - - - - - - - - - - - -

Vorführung des Schwimmwagens, Typ 128 beim Führer
und Generalfeldmarschall Keitel in der Reichskanzlei am

Während der Vorführung des Typ 128 bat ich den Führer
zwecks rascher Durchführungder aufgegebenen 30 Schwimmwagen um die Erteilung der Dringlichkeitsstufe (Sonderstufe). Der Führer meinte, dass sich dies wegen des
geringen Quantums schon machen liesse und er wandte
sich diesbezüglich an Generalfeldmarschall Keitel, der
die Zusicherung gab, dass er die Sonderstufe für den
Bau der Schwimmwagen zur Verfügung stellen werde.

Ich machte ihn darauf aufmerksam, dass die Bestellungen
über die Werkstoffe dieser Wagen infolge der Dringlich-
keit bereits in der Sonderstufe SS hinausgegangen seien,
worauf Generalfeldmarschall Keitel mir antwortete, dass
dies ja die Hauptsache sei.

VW/Porsche Type 166 (short version) on a test drive at the Lafatscher Joch in 1942.

VW/Porsche Type 166/ 15, rear view with propeller and high exhaust system, April 1942.

The pictures on these two pages show test drives conducted by army specialists.

Schwimmwagen 166 as a tracked vehicle.

A Schwimmwagen prototype displayed at the Führer's Headquarters in East Prussia, with Hitler, Himmler, Generaloberst Jodl and SS General Wolff.

Bericht über die auf Wunsch des Kolonialpolitischen
Amtes im Beisein des Herrn Ober-Baurat Suchanka aus-
geführte Erprobungsfahrt mit Typ O.166/2 bei Innsbruck.
(5.9. - 8.9.1942).

Die Erprobung erstreckte sich auf allgemeine Verwendungsmöglichkeit
des Typ O.166 in den Kolonien und wurden Fahrversuche im Sumpf, im
Gelände, sowie Steigungsmessungen durchgeführt.

## 1.) Sumpffahrversuch - 5.9.42:

In einem von Herrn Oberbaurat Suchanka ausgesuchten Sumpf,
welcher etwa den Uferverhältnissen der afrikanischen Flüsse
entspricht, wurden verschiedene Durchfahrversuche unternommen.

Fahren durch Sumpfgelände mit sog. grundlosen Boden ist für
Fahrzeuge jeder Art (Raupe, Radantrieb) ein kaum lösliches Problem, doch kann gesagt werden und dies zeigte sich bei dem Fahr-
versuch, dass der Typ O.166 durch sein geringes Gewicht, der
grossen Übersetzung, dem glatten Aufbau-Unterteil, wie auch der
grossen Bereifung 200/12 günstigste Verwendungsmöglichkeit auch
bei dieser Bodenbeschaffenheit aufweist.

Beim Einfahren in den Sumpf, welcher von weichem Boden durch
Schilf und Schlingpflanzen in einen schmutzigen Teich führt,
blieb der Wagen durch Rutzschen der Räder nach etwa 10 - 12 m
Fahrt stecken. Mit einem mitgeführten 20 m langen Hanfseil
(ein Hanfseil ist für diese Zwecke weitaus besser als ein Draht-
seil) konnte der Wagen durch Ziehen dreier Männer und Mitlaufen
der treibenden Räder gut an Land gebracht werden. Der Wagen sank
teilweise bis zur Freibordhöhe ein. Schneeketten bringen keine
Besserung. Durch Nachdrücken mit dem mitgeführten Ruder kann
gut nachgeholfen werden. Bei kurzen Sumpfein- und -ausfahrten
genügen aufgelegte Bretter. Geringer Reifendruck ist zu em-
pfehlen.

## 2.) Auffahrt zum Lavatscha-Joch (Übergang zum Karwendel) - 6.9.42:

Zu dem etwa 2000 m hohen Lavatscha-Joch wurde von Hall b/Inns-
bruck aus gefahren. Der Fussweg mit seinen Steigungen bis zu
etwa 60 % geht über Latschen, Steilhänge, Steinlawinen und fel-
sigen Boden in starken Spitzkehren bis zur Höhe. Die Auffahrt
wurde mit voller Belastung des Fahrzeugs (4 Personen) unternommen. Einige Male mussten 2 - 3 Personen abspringen, da die
Räder durchrutzschten, Motorgrenze erreicht wurde, oder aber
das Fahrzeug abzurutschen drohte und schnell gestützt werden
musste.

Recht stolz erreichten wir unser Ziel unter dem Beifall einiger
Touristen, die unsere Anfahrt beobachtet hatten und nicht glauben
konnten, dass wir bis oben kommen würden.

Trotz vollster Motor- und Fahrgestellbeanspruchung traten kei-
nerlei Störungen auf. (Motordeckel war geschlossen, keine
Benzinpumpenstörungen)

Bei Auffahrt betrug die Aussentemperatur 25 - 28°C. im Schatten.

Die Abfahrt verlief ohne Zwischenfälle.

An off-road VW "test car" (Porsche Type 92/82 E with high Kübelwagen chassis).

The interior of the off-road Beetle: simple Kübelwagen seats, wooden grids on the floor. The car belongs to a collector from Bielefeld.

An off-road Beetle with widened fenders.

A VW Type 92 stuck in the snow.

Test runs for the off-road Beetle on the factory grounds.

Off-road Beetle Type 92 SS: Two rifle racks in the back, with the first-aid kit behind them.

The seats of Type 92 SS fold down. On the floor to the right is a spare fuel can (with SS lettering). Built in 1943.

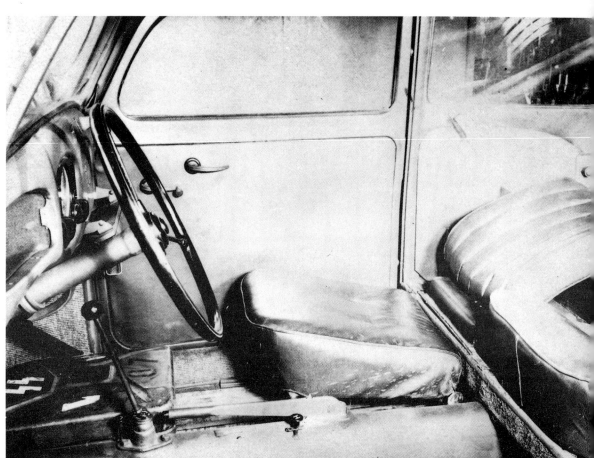

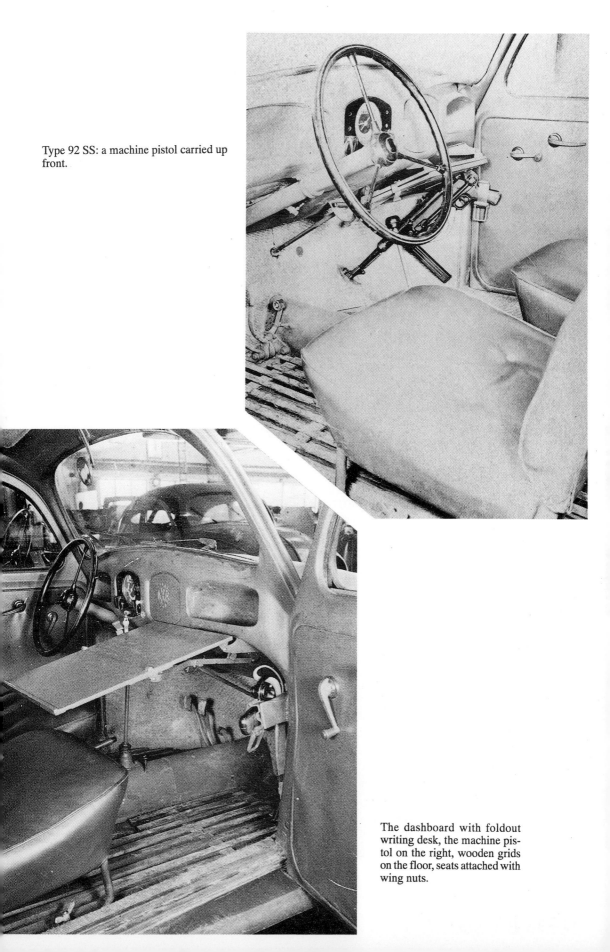

Type 92 SS: a machine pistol carried up front.

The dashboard with foldout writing desk, the machine pistol on the right, wooden grids on the floor, seats attached with wing nuts.

VW/Porsche Type 98 (Kabrio-Limousine with four-wheel drive). Widened fenders and running boards for the military off-road wheels. (October 1943)

Dashboard with writing desk, standard gearshift for 1st to 4th and reverse gears mounted high, as the shifting rod runs through the central tunnel (driveshaft for front wheels in tunnel). Second shift lever for front drive and off-road gear. Hand-brake lever to the side. Tunnel has screwed-on opening at the front.

A look through the opened roof panel at the three-seat interior.

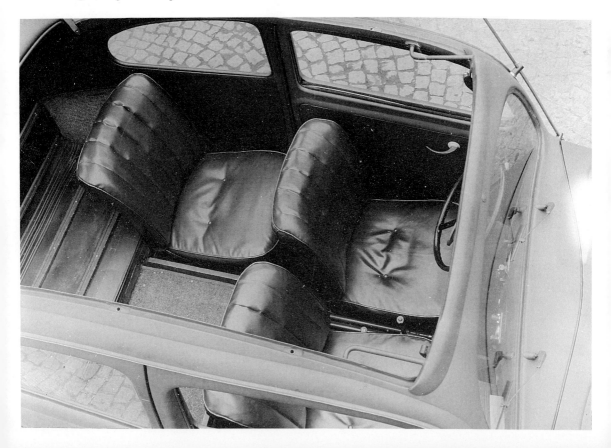

Engine compartment.
The blower duct and air
filter at the side are easy
to see. The car has
Stuttgart registration.

A look under the front hood of the Type
98: The wide spare wheel does not fit into
its space. Thus the fuel can is stored there,
and the spare wheel is kept in the luggage space above.

The rear seat of the three-seater. The two shift rods run above the tunnel.

The rear seat bench with the battery box opened.

The VW pickup on off-road chassis (Type 825). A hatch in the bed and two small doors give access to the motor. The rear panel can be unscrewed for servicing or replacing the motor.

VW box van as a test vehicle on the Autobahn (May 1941). The rear view with open door shows the motor under the bed. The carburetor is mounted to the side to gain space. This is the "tropical version."

# Running on Wood-Gas

The chronic gasoline shortage in Germany during World War II, resulting from limited importing of oil, made it necessary to promote alternatives.

Among the "native fuels" were petroleum obtained in Germany, as well as synthetic gasoline – made from coal, petroleum and vegetable matter. During the war, these two fuels were used only where less efficient fuels could not be used – thus almost exclusively in the Luftwaffe and on the front. In all other cases, especially for motor vehicles within Germany, the other available fuels were made use of: primarily the gases propane and butane, which were obtained from coal during the refining of gasoline and oil, and which could be liquefied easily under slight pressure. The steel bottles of these liquid gases were installed under the rear beds of trucks, or attached vertically to trailers.

There were even attempts made to convert the VW sedan to running on gas (Type 240). The gas bottle was installed horizontally beside the shortened rear seat and pushed through an opening into the engine compartment – a daring undertaking, as was soon to be shown: During test runs, one driver had a fatal accident when the gas bottle shot forward under heavy braking.

Another patented solution was running on wood-gas. Since Germany had been cut off totally from the world market for sources of energy and found itself with no sources of fuels, such antiquated recipes, applied to a limited extent, still proved to be quite useful.

The basis of all these considerations was the fact that in the Reich there were wood reserves in ample supply and evenly distributed – so there was enough material, and there were no transportation costs.

In the 1930s, Germans had looked into the future and placed great hopes on generator technology, which they developed accordingly. Automobiles with "Festgas Motor" were given tax breaks, and a bonus was granted of 600 RM for Diesel and 100 RM for gasoline engines to be converted to wood-gas. There were more than twenty manufacturers of generators in the German Reich, the best-known being the Imbert Generatoren GmbH of Cologne. In 1933 there were some 2500 vehicles running on wood-gas.

The Gustloff Works in Wiener Neustadt advertised their products in 1942-1943: "Motor vehicle generators promote motorization in wartime too. The Gustloff Works support this advance by an exemplary generator representing the newest state of technology. Years of scientific research and experiment created the prerequisites for a high-quality product which, through light weight and thus small consumption of material, simple installation and reliability, guarantee the economical operation of their utilitarian vehicles."

In fact, the generator technology was improved more and more, so that, as was stated in an article in the weekly magazine "Das Reich", edited by the Propaganda Minister, Dr. Goebbels, on December 29, 1940, not only beechwood but also "the low-value branch wood of pine can be used. Through the utilization of other gas-giving fuels such as turf, anthracite and coke, an overburdening of the heating market can be avoided." As liquid fuel became rarer and rarer toward the end of the war, about 80% of all German motor vehicles ran on wood-gas: cars and trucks, buses, tractors, towing vehicles and even tanks.

The generator was a large device in which the dried wood was converted into gas. It was mounted on the back of most cars, and between the cab and rear body of trucks. In order to make room on cars, the rear was simply cut off crudely. The VW with its rear engine was an exception here. The voluminous generator had to fit into the front, the appearance of which it almost totally ruined. And since it extended downward some distance, a large part of the useful ground clearance was lost.

Before the gas was ducted to the motor to be burned, it had to be cleaned and cooled. The water vapor contained in the gas was separated out in the cooler. A mixing valve on the motor added the air necessary for full combustion. The motor sucked in the necessary amount of mixture according to its speed. In the bottom of the oven were the wood coals, with the "fuel wood" on top. The wood coal lying in front of the air jets was ignited by a fuse through an air intake opening. The necessary suction was created by a blower or by the motor running on gasoline at first. After three or four minutes, the gas generation had proceeded to the extent that gasoline was no longer needed. What with the rather low heating power, the added air had to be set at the most beneficial rate. For that purpose, a lever had to be adjusted during driving. By increasing the compression conditions in the motor, adjusting the ignition point to the gas, which was not too willing to ignite, the decline in power could, ideally, be reduced to 20%. The actual generator, the gas cooler, settling tank, purifier, and necessary steel pipes as connectors (often running across the roof) and the sacks stuffed full of wood on the roof luggage rack – in short, the whole dreadful installations and additions – more or less misshaped the car. Additional coverings – giving the VW Beetle a streamlined nose like the Ford Eifel – improved the terrible appearance only a little.

Operating the generator was a difficult process and not for the nervous: technical knowledge, a calm nature, divine patience, a deep sensitivity to the spirit of the car and a stoic acceptance of soot and stink were required to drive a wood-burning car to a nearby destination at a top speed of 50 kph.

Even "filling her up" was a risky business. An auto magazine from Freiburg gave this suggestion in November 1947: "Before refueling, give full gas for about half a minute and suddenly turn off the ignition. Then move the air level to its closed position, quickly perform the servicing operations and, as usual, start by using the starter or by rolling downhill."

It was bad when the driver had forgotten to add a few pieces of wood at the right time, and if no wood coal was brought along to replenish the burned-down firebed. A word of advice on that: "At first fill in a level of 10 to 20 cm of wood or brown coal. Opel the filling cover and insert a piece of wood or the like into the vent flap so that air can enter freely. After some 30 to 40 minutes, fill with fuel. Close the cover, engage and start as usual."

No matter how happy the proud driver might be to drive his vehicle over the few smooth roads without shaking and jolting, it was not good for the gas-burning car to be treated too kindly. "When driving on the Autobahn and on roads that are in very good condition and do not shake the car much, the danger of incomplete combustion makes itself known in many wood-gas generators. So as not to have to get out and stoke the fire during a trip, it is recommended that in case of such 'autobahn bad-burners' one should drive on the pulloffs or parking areas found at large intervals on the Autobahn. The reason: These pulloffs or parking areas are usually paved in mosaic form, and the roadway generally has a small rut, necessary for water drainage, at the transition points for driving onto or off the actual Autobahn. Driving on this causes a slight shaking of the entire gas generator, which is sufficient to cause the wood to fall and thus eliminate the incomplete combustion. If the problem is eliminated too late, there is the danger that fuel containing tar will reach the burning area. In this case it soon becomes charcoal."

Shutting down in the evening was also a laborious and unpleasant procedure. Whoever still remembers the good old coal stove from home can imagine what it was like: Remove the ashes, clean the generator or poke up the contents of the shaft, etc. It was practical to let the generator burn over night, since the nightly evaporation of the fuel lying over the firebed would result in enough wood coal or brown coal briquette-coke forming, and thus no "fresh" fuel came to be near the jets. Whoever put the burning gas generator in the barn, workshop or garage overnight did well to use a flexible hose as an exhaust pipe to let the resulting gases escape through the chimney. And: "In the morning, to protect the battery, the generator is started by means of a portable blower that is connected to the electric power line."

Despite all of this grim reality, driving a car seems to have been friendlier in those gloomy times. Thus the passionate motorist was given the friendly advice: "Help each other! From a long way off, you can already recognize from the towering gas generator or the gas cooler attached to the front that the driver of the car stopped on the Autobahn with a flat tire is "one of the club." Stop and help as much as you can. Whether he needs some wood coal or fuel to get to the next filling station, or a connecting duct has broken and he needs a replacement duct to make emergency repairs, or the like. It should come as no surprise that a Berlin interzone traveler who had a flat tire on a lonely country road in Bavaria was lent a spare wheel by a Bavarian wood-gas driver so that, along with his rescuer, he could at least drive to the next flat-fixing shop. This example of true helpfulness should be a model for all of us!"

A great future was still promised to the wood-gas generator in 1947, for the gasoline shortage was still so great at that time that its rationing was not even sufficient for the most urgent use. Thus one could read in the already quoted Freiburg auto magazine: "The only alternative, even in the long run, is the increased use of generators in the transport economy and the utilization of fixed native fuels. These fuels are on German soil in inexhaustible quantities, do not cost much, and also play a role in creating employment. The fuel and generator problem is no minor part of the program of transport economy; it can only be regarded and decided within the framework of the entire economic policy. It is no particular stroke of luck that the great majority of our generator manufacturing factories stand ready to produce, nor that a conversion to generator power can be carried out quickly."

After the currency reform, the smoking and foul-smelling wood-gas generators soon disappeared from the scene. In the progressive 1950s with their pastel-colored and chrome-flashing cars, they were scrapped mercilessly. Thus not one of these early gas-bottle Volkswagens has survived the pressure of time. It would have been a choice morsel for any technical museum.

Volkswagen powered by bottled gas (Type 240), September 1943. The pictures show the gas bottle installed beside the rear seat, its covering, and its connection to the motor.

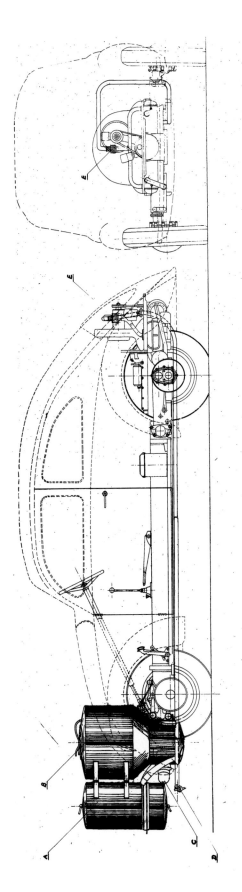

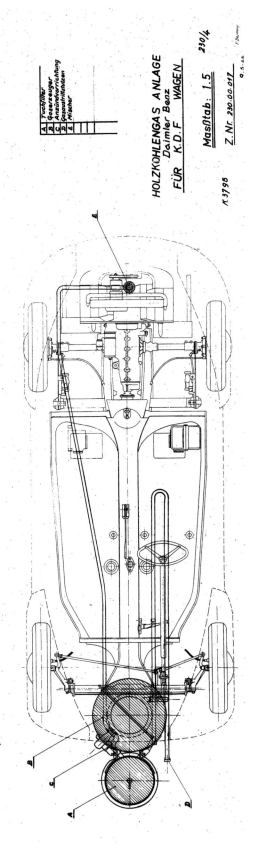

HOLZKOHLENGAS ANLAGE
Daimler Benz
FÜR K.D.F. WAGEN

| A | Tuchfilter |
| B | Gaserzeuger |
| C | Anzündevorrichtung |
| D | Gasauffüllnitzen |
| E | Mischer |

Maßstab: 1.5          230/4
K.3796
Z.Nr. 230.00.012
9.5.44

Plans for a Daimler-Benz wood-gas system for VW/Porsche Type 230/4, May 9, 1944. The following photo shows the car itself.

VW Type 92 with wood-gas generator by Daimler-Benz (Porsche Type 230), built in 1944.

Kübelwagen and off-road Beetle with gas generators ("test cars for native fuels").

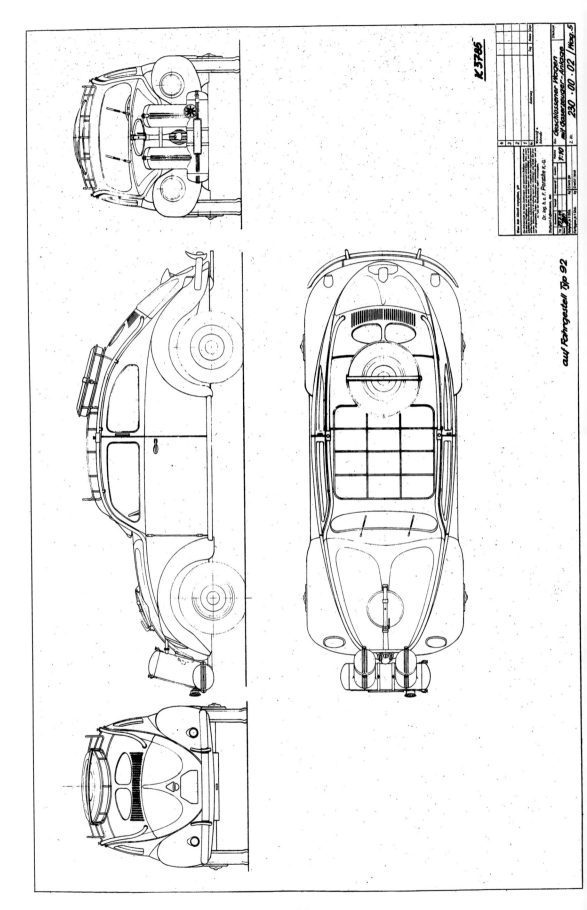

auf Fahrgestell Typ 92

K 3785

Geschlossener Wagen
mit Gaserzeuger-Anlage

Dr. Ing. h. c. F. Porsche K.-G.

Z. Nr. 230 . 00 . 02 / Wag. 5

74

The gas generator of this Porsche Type 230 has been covered by a streamlined front hood. A roof luggage rack with special spare tire holder was also made for this car. The "solid fuel" for these cars was carried in sacks on the roof rack. The factory building in the background is covered with camouflage nets. Below: the opened hood of the lengthened front end affords a view of the generator and strainer.

Front view of an off-road sedan with gas generator (Porsche Type 230), built in 1944. The hood is held by tension springs and is wide enough to provide space for the voluminous generator. With the hood open, the strainer can be seen behind the generator. As can be seen, the generator projects well below the bottom of the car, which is probably why the off-road VW with its high chassis was preferred.

# The Volkswagen in Action

The VW off-road sedan was accorded only a subsidiary role in wartime action, for too few of them had been built. On the other hand, the Kübelwagen saw service almost everywhere – it was the German Jeep. The Schwimmwagen was used from 1942 on, primarily by the reconnaissance units of the Panzer Grenadiers, especially the fast units of the Waffen-SS, the independently operating cycle rifle battalions serving as modern cavalry, for shock-troop undertakings, meaning the quick forward pushes of fast, mobile small attack units, for scouting in the country, fighting against pockets of enemy resistance, etc. Kübel- and Schwimmwagen were also used frequently as communication and fast courier vehicles. The lightness and great off-road capability of the VW proved to be unqualified advantages. On the muddy roads of Russia, even the Volkswagen got stuck often enough, but where other vehicles had long since given up, it kept plodding forward through a deep morass. In addition, the VW, thanks to its air-cooling and oil cooler, was insensitive to extreme climates. After a cold winter night, a Mercedes Kübel, for example, had to be brought back to life with blow-lamps, hot water or a gasoline fire under the engine block. Often it was sufficient to start the VW by simply cranking or pushing it. The VW Kübel was also resistant to hot desert climate. It was able to handle the strains of the Russian and African campaigns simply by being cranked or pushed.

It turned out to be a big plus that the simply built Volkswagen could usually be repaired with the few tools carried on board, that parts could be exchanged thanks to the relatively great numbers of Volkswagens, and that the spare-parts service functioned relatively well. Another incalculable advantage was the maneuverability of the little Volkswagen in heavy column traffic, in jammed-up tight places, at bridges and fords, in the jumble of tracked and wheeled vehicles, towing tractors, guns, horse-drawn wagons, troops, etc.

One comment about paint: The Reichswehr used gray-green-brown camouflage until 1935, the Wehrmacht dark gray-dark green from then until the war began. From 1940 on, a monotone dark gray was prescribed. As the war spread, various instructions were given for the various theaters of war.

According to instructions of March 17, 1941, the vehicles of the Afrika-Korps were to be sprayed with yellow-brown paint (RAL 8000); camouflage patterns with flowing transitions were to be applied with gray-green paint (RAL 7008). Since the Afrika-Korps was set up in great haste in order to come to the aid of the endangered Italian Army and no tropical paint was available in Germany in 1941, dark gray vehicles were often smeared with a lime solution on the spot for the sake of simplicity, in order to make them match the desert colors. Since it was necessary to be sparing with paint, the old gray basic color was generally left on and yellow-brown paint added in spots of camouflage. Under the extreme conditions of the desert climate, the paint of the vehicles naturally suffered. The bright sunlight caused much bleaching and flaking of the paint. A sandstorm with the effect of a sandblaster could take off the paint down to the bare metal. The troops could made do with captured British supplies at times, but there were constant shortages there. In any case, there was no uniform paint color for the Afrika-Korps.

At the beginning of the Russian campaign, almost all Wehrmacht vehicles were painted uniform gray. When the winter war began, a coating of washable winter camouflage paint was ordered. But since such chalky paint was available only in limited quantities because of the supply problem, it was often smeared on in spots or stripes with a twig broom or "painted" in short brush strokes. Sometimes whitewash was also used. Near Russian villages or in places where the snowy landscape was not plain white without vegetation, this was sufficient to blur the contours of the vehicle. With the spring offensive of 1942 in the directions of Stalingrad, Maikop and Baku, the usual dark gray Wehrmacht paint was enhanced with a dark green spot camouflage. In the southern part of the Russian front (Caucasus, Crimea) there were naturally numerous sand-colored vehicles as well.

Instructions dated February 18, 1943 introduced a new paint system. Since the dark gray paint had not produced the desired camouflage effect, the change was made to a dark yellow basic color. The additional camouflage colors were now olive green and red-brown. The units were free to choose their own camouflage patterns. The result was a bizarre confusion of colors. The reasons for this may be sought in supply problems for one thing, and for another in the paint itself, which could be mixed with either water or gasoline. When applied mixed with water, the new camouflage paint could scarcely stand up to a rainstorm. Even in the next drizzle or fog. they ran down the vehicle in small streams. Only when thinned with gasoline were they resistant. But since gasoline was in short supply everywhere, either the paint was thinned too little or efforts were made to thin it with used oil, with the result that the paint turned color: green turned to black, brown to red.

As long as the German Luftwaffe was superior in the air, the Wehrmacht rarely felt the need to camouflage its vehicles with branches. This changed with the war situation in 1942-1943, but even more so with the American invasion of Normandy in June 1944. Since the Allies now held complete air superiority over France, German reserves could be moved to the invasion front in daylight only when well camouflaged. In order to obscure the outlines of the vehicles, they were camouflaged with tree branches, evergreen twigs or bundles of straw. Some of the pictures in this book show this.

The deteriorating supply situation meant that not only camouflage paint was lacking more and more, but so were spare parts and tires for repair. And since the German troops in the east were more and more involved in losing battles, at least since 1943, there was scarcely time for vehicle maintenance. In the front-line repair shops, only makeshift repairs were made, or damaged vehicles were cannibalized, in order to keep their time out of action short. As a rule, the life span of a vehicle lasted only three weeks. Under these conditions it would have been sheer waste to carry on intensive maintenance. The German military vehicles of 1944-1945 thus made a miserable impression: bashed and bent body panels, missing parts, wrong wheels and tires, etc. Only a few specimens used at training camps in Germany could have looked spotless during the war, as the restored Kübel- and Schwimmwagen appear at veterans' gatherings today.

Many a Volkswagen was simply left by the roadside as the German troops retreated. Many vehicles were abandoned for lack of gasoline, while others were left as wrecks on the battlefield or after air attacks. Depending on opportunity and need, German rear guards may have taken them, and naturally the opposing forces and civilians appropriated them too, as happened along the Allied advance routes.

The Japanese ambassador in front of the embassy in Berlin. The VW has a Japanese flag and CD license on the front. On the left fender is the camouflage headlight, obligatory during the war.

The VW sedan was delivered chiefly to factory officials and government or party agencies during the war, and generally used for display or testing. This VW Beetle has wartime headlight coverings and a camouflage light on the left fender.

For the colonial office in the foreign ministry, two off-road Beetles on the Kübelwagen chassis were built in 1941 (clearly recognizable by the high position). The cars had gloss paint, chromed bumpers, a klaxon horn on the side, and were driven to Afghanistan in convoy with other vehicles.

The two Afghanistan Beetles ready to start in Berlin and (next page, top) in a Balkan city.

The VW Beetle in Budapest, 1941.

*Der KdF-Wagen (in Friedensausführung) vor dem Alten Museum, Berlin*

# Kraft durch Freud

8. JAHRGANG · NUMMER 5 · 1. MAI 1941 · 10 PFEN

# Auch er fährt mit gegen Engelland.

Er — nämlich der KdF.-Wagen — den wir auf unserem Bild in seinem feldgrauen Kleide fast nicht erkannt hätten, und den wir hier als treuen Helfer der Luftwaffe vor zweitausendjährigen Tempelruinen auf Sizilien sehen. Herr Churchill hätte sich gewiß nicht träumen lassen, daß er durch seinen Rundfunk längst totgesagten KdF.-Wagen so schnell schon begegnen würde. In unerschütterlichem Vertrauen zu „ihrem KdF.-Wagen" sparen gerade jetzt Hunderttausende von Volksgenossen unbeirrbar weiter, in der Hoffnung, ihn recht bald nach siegreich beendetem Kriege zu erhalten. Dies beweist auch nebenstehendes im Auszug veröffentlichte Schreiben, das wir von einem z. Zt. in Afrika stehenden Soldaten erhalten haben.

An die NSG. „Kraft durch Freude"     Afrika, im Mö
Gaudienststelle Berlin

Heute erhielt ich von Ihnen eine Aufrechnung über abge
Sparkarten usw. . . . Hoffentlich befriedigt mic
KdF.-Wagen nachher genau so, wie heute als
wagen hier in der großen Wüste.     Heil Hitler!

Heinz T . . , Oberg

Libya, 1942: A Kübelwagen crew talks to a native. The Via Balbia was the only blacktopped road in Cyrenaica.

Two Afrika-Korps Kübelwagen. Note the two spare wheels on the front hood.

Loading the vehicles in Naples.

A motorized reconnaissance unit marches into Benghazi (1941).

This Kübelwagen with its usual dark green paint was smeared with lime to match the color of the desert. The lime is already flaking off in many places. Even the windshield was smeared with lime to reduce the glare of the sunlight. The top was usually not treated, as the flapping of the canvas made the lime break off quickly. The driver's helmet hangs over the headlight. On the fender is the symbol of the Afrika-Korps, a palm tree with swastikas.

A VW driver observes the skies. This Kübel also had its regular green color covered with lime.

The crew of this Luftwaffe Kübel, seen near Tunis, is looking for mines on a scouting trip.

A VW Kübelwagen as a dummy tank, used by the Afrika-Korps. Such vehicles were often used by Rommel for deceptive maneuvers.

Cycle riflemen in a new Kübelwagen at the Heuberg training camp in the spring of 1941. 15th Company, "Nordland" Regiment. Note the shield around the windshield.

Linez, October 16, 1941: a barn is used for cover and as a garage.

Schirdra position, August 1942. In the background is a Russian farm building set afire by enemy bombing.

Being checked by a Feldjäger.

The Kübelwagen of a weapons and radio master.

The supplies of white camouflage paint were usually limited. Thus this Kübel was painted only sparingly with spots and swirls. With this crude paint job, the vehicle scarcely stands out from the black-gray-white landscape with its snow and bushes.

Eastern front, winter 1941. Two medium Uniform Pkw have been smeared or sprayed with chalk paint. The VW Kubel still lacks winter camouflage.

The combat around Husiatynm Ukraine, in the summer heat of July 1941. The pictures give an impression of the demands made on man and machines.

Motorized scouting troops of the Waffen-SS (Leibstandarte Adolf Hitler) with Kübelwagen at the edge of Cherson.

Pictures taken by an SS correspondent (propaganda company), published in "Das Schwarze Korps", July 29, 1943. "The swimming Volkswagen surmounts every obstacle. The march goes through cornfields, over slopes and valleys or through rivers and lakes."

"In the roadless areas, the motorcycle riflemen are not equipped with rifles, but with the Volkswagen." (Original title, Schwarze Korps, 3/18/1943)

SS grenadiers drive a camouflaged VW onto a bridge, hoping to capture it in a surprise attack and gain a crossing.

"The Schwimmwagens, camouflaged with tent canvas and branches, approach the enemy shore." (Schwarze Korps, 10/28/1943)

The pictures, showing a reconnaissance unit of the Waffen-SS, were published in "Das Schwarze Korps:, Sept. 9, 1943, captioned: "The light cavalry of today." "The nimble off-road Swim-Volkswagen also belongs to the reconnaissance units."

Above: A driver makes a report.

Below: Captured Russians are searched for weapons.

Upper right, next page: Soviet forces go into battle.

Eastern front, Oct.-Nov. 1943:
The hard defensive fighting is
in progress. At the wheel of this
VW is Knight's Cross (with
oak leaves) holder SS
Sturmbannführer Georg
Bochmann.

A Schwimmwagen of a reconnaissance unit, camouflaged with swirls of paint.

A VW amphibian Kübel of the 72nd Infantry Division Staff 266) with remarkable camouflage; winter 1944-1945.

The original gray paint of this Schwimmwagen in Russia was simply sprayed with yellow spots. A curious feature of this Volkswagen is the exhaust system above the rear, outside the body. An oar and a shovel are attached to the side. The headlights have the usual covers with slits. The car has normal VW wheels.

A dusty Kübelwagen of the Afrika-Korps (palm symbol on the door). The WL lettering indicates a Luftwaffe vehicle. Easy to see are the covered headlights, camouflage light beside the spare wheel, directional signals on the windshield frame, and the horn on the door. The shovel is fastened to the right side of the car. The tactical symbol is seen on the left front fender. Look closely and note the different tires.

Motorized troops of the "Wiking" SS Division on the Russian plains in the summer of 1941. This Schwimmwagen's spare wheel is covered by a swastika flag to show the Luftwaffe where the spearhead of the German attack is. Russian prisoners sit among the German soldiers.

A reconnaissance trip on the broad plains of Russia, with two Kübelwagen.

Russia, summer 1943. A Schwimmwagen of the SS Panzer Division "Das Reich."

A Waffen-SS patrol with VW Schwimmwagen.

Reichsmarschall Hermann Goering inspects Luftwaffe Kübelwagen.

The General of the Panzer Troops, Heinz Guderian (saluting at left) takes leave of General Paulus (in back seat of Mübelwagen), Chief Quartermaster I in the Army high command for the Panzer Troops.

Felix Steiner, General of the Waffen-SS, is also traveling in a Kübelwagen.

A Luftwaffe celebration, with officers taking a tour of honor. (BA)

Away from the grim reality of war: a test drive with a Schwimmwagen at the bend of the Dniester. The 97th Jäger Division with the "rooster feather" division symbol originally had the seat of its division staff in Bad Tölz, Bavaria.

A Waffen-SS unit withdrawing, spring 1943. A VW Kübel between two Schützenpanzerwagen, at left are two "Maultier" halftrack trucks, in the background behind the motorcycle is a VW Schwimmwagen.

Cycle riflemen of the 9th Panzer Division pass a Büssing-NAG 8-ton truck. Photographed near Kiev, September 1941.

Withdrawal to the Bug, spring 1944: two VW Kübel, a Steyr 1500 A and a Büssing-NAG 4.5-ton truck.

Beside the mighty Büssing-NAG Type BN 9 halftrack towing vehicle, the little VW Kübelwagen looks like a toy. Panzer-Grenadier Division "Grossdeutschland."

With its two-wheel drive, the Kübelwagen was at a disadvantage compared to any four-wheel-drive military vehicles. Still in all, even situations like this could be handled.

Autumn mud in Russia!

Schwimmwagen of a recon-
naissance unit in action on the
eastern front, winter 1943. The
vehicles are equipped with tire
chains.

A Schwimmwagen entering the water.

The deployment of fast troops used to be done on horseback; in modern warfare it is motorized. Here we see cavalry and motorized units with Volkswagens side by side in Russia.

A Schwimmwagen of the 205th Infantry Division.

Driving school at a training camp, with Kübel,
Schwimmwagen and halftrack towing tractor.

When there is no jack handy, use a chuck of wood!

If need be, the Schwimmwagen can be moved by muscle power!

Transport problems are solved! A VW on a Schützenpanzerwagen, summer 1943, during transfer of the 1st SS Panzer Division from the eastern front to Italy.

Both pictures below show the transfer of an SS reconnaissance unit from Greece to Romania, by rail and on their own wheels, in 1944.

A Kübel in the desert. The dashboard panel with speedometer is easy to see. Safety boxes are on either side of it. Thick-spoked steering wheel. A photo from the Netherlands edition of the German propaganda journal "Signal."

Dr. Porsche with a test car in Prague, 1943.

The communications vehicles struggle to move forwards on the roads, which turned into a sea of mud in the melting season.

The reconnaissance unit of the "Leibstandarte Adolf Hitler" moves forward for a counterattack on March 6, 1943.

July 11, 1943: A reconnaissance unit pushes into Vassilievka. The motorcycle riflemen jump out while the cars are in motion and go on the offensive.

A Schwimmwagen of the 3rd SS Panzer Division.

The men of a telephone company on the road with their Volkswagen. ("Das Reich" Division).

Wrecked vehicles after an air attack.

The notorious SS Obergruppenführer Theodor Eicke, commander of the SS Totenkopf Division on the eastern front, gets into his VW Kübelwagen.

A shock troop of the Waffen-SS in action with two Kübelwagen.

A Volkswagen Kübel captured by the Russians. The markings include Cyrillic letters. Photographed in Vilna, July 1944.

Photographed at Nettuno, Italy, in 1944, a VW Kübel makes way for a Schützenpanzerwagen bringing wounded men to the rear.

The Waffen-SS on parade in Paris in 1942.

A Wehrmacht column with a Schwimmwagen crosses the border between Menton (France) and Monaco in 1943. (BA)

A Schwimmwagen pack in Toulon in 1943.

Pictures from German-occupied Monaco; above, in front of the famous gambling casino; below, on the coast road.

Open roads could be covered only one jump at a time when well camouflaged. Original caption: "The long, endless columns of our attacking reserves roll forward nonstop on the roads of Normandy toward the beach-heads of the Anglo-Americans." Photographed June 8, 1944, two days after the invasion began.

The Allied air superiority over France in 1944 made every daylight trip a life-threatening adventure.

A shot-down and burning vehicle column including Volkswagens.

"Refugees in Normandy. The stream of heavily loaded refugee wagons and carts on the roads leading out of the combat area gets nowhere." (original caption)

Invasion front, 1944: SS divisions brought from
Russia are in the midst of the combat against newly-
landed Anglo-American units. Soldiers of an SS unit
with a Schwimmwagen counterattacking in the
Caen area.

Western front: a paratroop unit's Schwimmwagen camouflaged with branches.

Invasion front, 1944: A rather battered Schwimmwagen in a suburb of Caen. The front of the car is covered with a camouflage net. The vehicle shows clear signs of damage.

Invasion area, 1944: Assault Gun III on the march to the front, led by a VW followed by a motorcycle messenger.

The crew of a Schwimmwagen salute as they leave for the front in the west, autumn 1944.

The Kübelwagen of a Panzergrenadier regiment on the invasion front in 1944.

A camouflaged Kübel leaves the grounds of the former Ardenne Cloister northwest of Caen. The tactical symbol on the fender indicates the 12th SS Panzer Division "Hitlerjugend." Summer 1944.

A Schwimmwagen of the 6th Panzer Army (Waffen-SS) during the German Ardennes Offensive between Malmedy and St. Vith, December 1944.

The SS attacks British airborne troops near Arnhem.

An Army Schwimmwagen in a wintry pine forest in 1944.

If need be, six soldiers could squeeze into a cramped Schwimmwagen! 78th Infantry and Assault Division, Christmas 1944.

A VW Kübelwagen crosses a river in the Weserbergland on a ferry, spring 1945.

British airborne troops cross the Rhine in a captured Kübelwagen, March 1945.

American soldiers inspect a captured VW Kübelwagen of the Waffen-SS. Note the different tires, typical of the tire shortage in Germany toward the end of the war. A scene from the Ardennes Offensive, December 1944.

A town on the western front, spring 1945, with German and American soldiers beside a Luftwaffe Kübelwagen.

Invasion front, 1944: A Volkswagen captured by Americans.

Bülow Street, Berlin, July 1944, after an air raid. A KdF-Wagen (VW Type 60) drives past a damaged elevated line.

Vienna, early April 1945: The city has been declared a defensive area. Waffen-SS units have set up barricades on the exit roads. On April 10 the Soviets pushed into the city. The last of Vienna's German defenders left the city via the only break in the Russian lines, on the Florisdorf Bridge. Above: Between the sentries and the destroyed streetcars is a Kuubelwagen. Below: A Wehrmacht column with VW, Opel and Ford trucks.

Berlin, May 1945: In the courtyard of the Reich Chancellery is a shot-up Volkswagen (off-road Beetle 82 E).

Berlin right after the city surrendered. Amid the wreckage of the German Army, homeless people seek the necessities of life. Among the abandoned and destroyed vehicles are desolate Kübel- and Schwimmwagen.

# Wolfsburg 1945-1946

Despite the desperate efforts made to defend the homeland, catastrophe reached Germany unstoppably in the spring of 1945. Between January 12, when the Soviets opened their major offensive on the entire eastern front, and April 12, when the American armies crossed the Elbe, the German Wehrmacht suffered a complete defeat. In January and February the Russians overran East and West Prussia and also occupied the industrial region of Upper Silesia (the only German industrial area that had remained mostly unharmed by bombing until then). Early in March, the exhausted German forces were still able to delay the Red Army at the Oder for a time, but on March 16 this last great German defensive position broke under the attack of the far superior Russian armies. By the end of February, the Anglo-American forces had put pressure on the Rhine front, and they crossed the Rhine on March 7. On March 6 Cologne was captured, on March 29 Frankfurt. On April 1 a German army group was surrounded in the Ruhr area. On April 9 the 9th U.S. Army took Hannover and crossed the Autobahn to Braunschweig. On April 11, US troops reached the Elbe near Magdeburg.

The war machine of the enemy powers was now rolling toward the Volkswagen city too. On April 5, scattered German units appeared on the Fallersleber Chaussee; they were harried, exhausted, completely inadequately armed, and went off to the east. On the next day, weapons were distributed to the local Volkssturm; the remaining food rations were divided among the population. On Monday, April 9, the sound of gunfire was heard from the Hannover area. All 47 men of the Volkssturm reported for service. Then it was decided not to defend the city of the KdF-Wagen and to disband the Volkssturm. Pictures of party leaders, maps and the like were burned. On Wednesday, April 11, all the remaining German units were withdrawn. The garrison and the local SS command disappeared. The rumor went around that American divisions had crossed the Mittelland Canal in the vicinity and were advancing. All resistance appeared to be useless. The staff of the VW Works (9000 at that time) were sent home. In this situation, filled with anxiety, grim forebodings and a latent sense of panic, things happened fast. The situation changed by the hour. The forces of order were completely disrupted.

The prisoners of war and forced laborers – Russians, Poles, Italians and French – stormed the arsenals of the departed German units. A food column was stormed by Germans and foreigners at the edge of town. On Thursday, April 12, the first US tank rolled into the city around noon. In the stores, the foreigners dipped their flags to greet the Americans.

In the next few days there were plundering, shooting and violence toward the German population. The increased tension burst forth. There were dead all over. German families fled into the nearby woods for fear of being overpowered by the now-free forced laborers. Attempts were made to set up a police force, since no troops had arrived yet. As far as possible, the work force was organized. But the chaos could no longer be controlled; looting of the supply stores, particularly supplies of potatoes in the country, the shops and houses went on unstopped. The Russians set up so-called "courts of blood" and murdered anyone they did not want. French prisoners of war and Hollanders attacked Poles and Russians with the watchword "Save Western Europe!" The Tullio-Cianetti Hall was destroyed senselessly. A pastor and the leader of the press corps turned to the US forces in Fallersleben to request a regular occupation of the KdF city because of the unrest, looting and violent attacks of all kinds. On Wednesday, April 18, the Americans finally moved in. Total confusion and a wild mixture of people prevailed. The Germans no longer dared to set foot on the streets.

On April 20, the Nazi big shots assembled once more in the Führer's bunker under the Reich Chancellery in Berlin on the occasion of Hitler's 56th birthday. Not yet convinced of the obvious hopelessness of the situation and still impressed by optimistic evaluations of the situation, Adolf Hitler was still convinced that the last bastions of the Greater German Reich could be held at the gates of Berlin and the war could be decided in Germany's favor. On April 21 he sent a telegram of thanks to Mussolini: "My thanks to you, Duce. The struggle that we wage for our bare existence has reached its high point . . . In the spirit of tough contempt for death, the German people and all who are of the same spirit will bring this storming to a stop, however hard the fight may be, and will change the course of the war through their unique heroism. At this historic moment, in which the fate of Europe will be decided for centuries to come, I send you my heartiest greetings. Adolf Hitler." On the eastern front, the Wehrmacht, Waffen-SS and Volkssturm still fought against the Red Army with all their might until the day of surrender.

On this day, the job of cleaning up the Volkswagen city began. The uniform salary was 80 Pfennig per hour.

The American forces originally had the intention of blowing up the volkswagen factory. The factory leadership met for daily conferences. The factory chief, Rudolf Brörmann, protested against the planned destruction. He had a Kübelwagen assembled out of available parts and tried to convince the Americans of its advantages. Rudolf Brörmann (1891-1957) had been a chief inspector at Opel before the war and had known the later VW chief Heinrich Nordhoff there. Nordhoff directed the truck branch in Brandenburg where the renowned Opel Blitz trucks were built. Brörmann had worked at the main plant in Rüsselsheim but moved to VW in 1938, where he again served as chief engineer. During the war he was given assignments at the Peenemünde rocket test center involving V-2 production, for which the Volkswagen Works produced parts. As opposed to present-day statements from the VW Works, Brörmann had never been in the USA. Although he was a party member, Rudolf Brörmann was said to be anti-fascistic in sentiment, as well as a very independent personality. He often had disagreements with the factory leadership, with Porsche and the party leaders. Under these conditions, Brörmann's cooperation with the Americans and British could not last for long. The British soon threw him out when they got fed up with his independent nature. The factory chief's membership in the Nazi Party was reason enough.

The fact that the VW Works were not blown up in the spring or summer of 1945 is attributable to Rudolf Brörmann. He constantly advocated that the production of motor vehicles be resumed. The VW Works has scarcely thanked him for that. Brörmann struggled long and unsuccessfully to rehabilitate himself. The factory has laid a blanket of silence over this epoch, and the official history of the firm begins only in 1948 with the arrival of Heinrich Nordhoff.

With his characteristic vanity and arrogance, Nordhoff always took full credit for the new beginning and rebuilding. In fact, though, the major damage had long since been repaired and production been brought back to a high level when the new man arrived in 1948. This does not diminish Nordhoff's contribution to the further prosperity of the factory, but it makes clear that others did the actual work of rebuilding under incredible difficulties in the three years from 1945 to 1947.

Nordhoff never acknowledged these contributions. The lordly demeanor and the vulgar arrogance of this man were quickly noticed by his predecessors. When Brörmann wanted to ask him for a job in the customer service department in 1948, the high and mighty new boss of VW made him wait in vain for five hours. Then Brörmann left, resigned to his fate.

However that may have been, at least the victors were interested in the remarkable car that they had already met when they captured vehicles in the war. On May 8, British officers, Colonel Radclyffe and Major Hirst, inspected the factory. On that day the famous competition between a VW Schwimmwagen and an American Jeep took part, which the VW won resoundingly. Brörmann convinced Radclyffe of the Volkswagen's advantages and the factory's ability to deliver it. Thereupon the British Army of the Rhine issued a contract for more than 20,000 vehicles.

In May and June of 1945, attempts were made to counteract the chaotic confusion and build up a planned regimen by establishing a city government and a responsible factory leadership. But the unstable personnel and work conditions, which were changed almost every day on the part of the Allies, made almost any orderly leadership impossible for a long time. The German executives who were called in soon departed as if through a revolving door. Within a few days, city officials and work forces were suspended from service, arrested and then returned to their old positions, only to be locked up again in the end.

On May 22, Rudolf Brörmann was named chief of the factory, and he was installed officially on May 28. At this time the first meeting of the city government, appointed by the American city commander, a first lieutenant, took place. The city officials decided to rename the city "Wolfsburg", as to date (May 25) it had still been called "Stadt des KdF-Wagens" officially.

A technical draftsman named Kern provided the design for the city's coat of arms: a castle gate with a stylized wolf and wavy lines, which symbolized the Mittelland Canal. The name of the city was taken from the Renaissance castle of Wolfsburg, which had been owned by the Counts von der Schulenburg since 1742. At the beginning of June, the new name was acknowledged orally by the chief of government, Freiherr von Heintze, and the head of the district council, Landrat Thomas, on their visit to the city officials. The name was sanctioned at the second meeting (June 22) of the city assembly appointed by the occupying forces.

On Sunday, June 3, the British took over the occupation of the city. The looting and destruction went on as before, and there were dead and badly injured victims again and again. In mid-June, efforts were made to send the children to school again, but instruction remained forbidden for the time being. Under the direction of their teachers, the children had to do cleaning-up work in the city and collect potato beetles.

Vehicle production had already been resumed in May, to be interrupted only for a few days. During that month, 110 Kübelwagen were assembled out of available parts. They were delivered to the 9th US Army. Under and amid the rubble there were still several half-finished vehicles and numerous chassis and bodies. But it was still impossible to achieve a deliberate increase of production and activity. The hesitant and halfhearted measures that were taken were scarcely an expression of a constructive concept, but rather a provisional approach. Until 1947, rebuilding, repairing and rehabilitation of buildings and machinery were still forbidden officially, for only in that year was the decision against dismantling the works finally made.

According to information from the occupying forces, the VW Works were originally to be used only as a repair shop for their own military vehicles. But since there was a great need for motor vehicles among both the Allies and the German officials, on account of the high losses in the war, the decision was made to produce automobiles (for the time being).

Another important reason existed: The Wolfsburg area was a gathering place for all sorts of controversial people: former forced laborers of various nations, German and foreign prisoners of war, refugees from the East, Communists, Nazis and westerners congregated there side by side, either in the open or in endless groups of barracks. Among the Germans, the trauma of the totally lost war, the gloom of self-awareness and the hopeless situation led to depressive effects; among the foreigners, the effects of long-term imprisonment were now unleashed in brutal acts of aggression in the streets of Wolfsburg. The shattered official consciousness was accessible to new ideological movements at any time in this catastrophic situation. Opportunistic and unprincipled behavior had appeared in 1945, and even before, resulting in surprising political changes. There was also a danger in Wolfsburg because it was near the border of the Soviet occupation zone. Among the British, who set the tone, there gradually developed the awareness that they had to counteract the very tense social situation. But without the VW Works it was impossible to create work and food. It was thus tactical cleverness on the part of the local authorities to oppose the demolition and also oppose the French demands for reparations.

It speaks well of the courage to improvise, the energetic desire to rebuild, resilient patience and massive efforts of the people that, in the catastrophic economic and technical conditions – lacking materials, sources of energy, transport capacity, skilled workers, cash reserves and the like – and with permanently disillusioning and depressing disagreements and quarrels with the authorities of the occupying powers and the constant confusion of the most contradictory regulations, a modest but continuing and growing vehicle production could be initiated. According to information from the VW Works, there were built in 1945:

| | |
|---|---|
| January 1-April 10 | 4330 Kübelwagen |
| May | 110 vehicles |
| June | 85 vehicles |
| July | 188 vehicles |
| August | 161 vehicles |
| September | 205 vehicles |
| October | 212 vehicles |
| November | 421 vehicles |
| December | 403 vehicles |

Thus by the end of 1945, 1785 Volkswagens had been built. Produced from May to December were:

| | |
|---|---|
| 669 | Type 51 (former type 92/82 E) off-road Beetles |
| 520 | Type 21 (former Type 82) Kübelwagen |
| 275 | Type 83 off-road Beetles with box body (mail trucks) |
| 225 | Type 28 Kübelwagen with box body (mail trucks) |
| 57 | Type 11 normal Beetles (former Type 60 KdF-Wagen) |
| 6 | Type 70 (former Type 166) Schwimmwagen, of spare parts |
| 3 | Type 27 Kübelwagen with pickup body |

In January 1946, 55 off-road Beetles and one Kübelwagen were built. The last high-clearance Beetle on the Kübelwagen chassis was finished January 29, 1946. In all, 1260 off-road Beetles (sedans and delivery vans) were built in 1945-1946. One single specimen was the normal Type 11 sedan built for Director Brömann on October 22, 1945, for only one pair of normal front half-axles was available. These parts only became available again as of December 1945, so that a few more examples could be finished by the end of the year. Director Brömann passed the car on to Colonel Radclyffe. In December the factory had a work force of 6033 people.

In 1946 the production of vehicles was increased considerably: In January, 875 cars were completed. In the following months, production increased to 1000. The goal announced by Brömann of 3000 cars a month by the end of the year could not be attained because of general shortages.

The considerable variations in the sale prices show that a rational price calculation was simply not possible. Until the end of March, the standard sedan cost 4150 RM; as of April the price rose to 5000 RM, staying there through June, then as of July it was reduced to 4000 RM, only to rise to 5000 RM again in December.

The increased production at the Wolfsburg works, to be sure, did little to ease the general transportation problems in destroyed Germany, for only a very small fraction of the new Volkswagens came into German hands. Only on August 9, 1946 were the first Beetles delivered to German agencies in the British Zone. At this time, no cars were yet sold to private customers.

Supplying the market with new cars for reconstruction would have been a blessing, for a transport crisis of the highest order was already crippling the simplest measures from the start. The railroad tracks and rolling stock were almost completely destroyed, the shipping lanes blocked by obstacles such as blown-up bridges, the freight barges and harbor facilities were largely destroyed by bombing. Since almost all available trucks had been sent to the fronts and lost, and even the fuel and spare-parts supply was quite insufficient, there was a shortage of suitable means of road transit everywhere. In addition, the roads, especially the Autobahnen, had been destroyed by bombing and blowing up bridges during the battles at the war's end. The depressing effects were painfully obvious to all during the winter of 1946-1947. While the coal supplies in the Ruhr area grew to ever-greater heights, thousands of people in other parts of Germany were freezing because the heating material could not be brought to where it was urgently needed.

The tense transport situation made it absolutely necessary to rebuild available cars into trucks, though this could usually be done only in individual cases. In general the process consisted of cutting off the bodies of any still-usable sedans behind the driver's seat, down to the level of the wheel wells, and building on a box or canvas-covered rear body. This often resulted in the strangest creations – without regard for the stability of the bodywork. The venerable old Opel, Adler, Mercedes, DKW and other cars of the 1930s were thus rebuilt and reshaped in large numbers.

It was naturally clear to transport specialists that these antiquated vehicles had to be replaced by new ones as soon as possible. Therefore several manufacturers put rebuilt cars into series production after the war. Daimler-Benz, for example, produced the first postwar Mercedes of all, the 170 V delivery van, as of May 1946 – it was an extremely primitive vehicle with a cab and doors made of wood.

The VW people also made efforts to make the two remaining original Volkswagens, the Kübel and the Beetle, suitable for the greatest variety of transport tasks of German government agencies, especially the postal and medical systems.

In the process, the cars did not become any better-looking, for some of them had a very bulky wooden or sheet-metal box body added, but these strange-looking vehicles were certainly useful in that time of poverty and shortages. In all, 500 Volkswagens with box bodies were built for the postal system: 225 Type 28 Kübelwagen and 275 Type 83 Beetles. Deliveries to the postal system began in September 1945 and ended in December. An ambulance with a box body was also built for various medical services. Since the box was too short to carry a lying patient, the head end of the stretcher projected into the cab. Thus the passenger seat had to be removed.

For the Reichspost VW the factory made a single-axle trailer (Type 93). When a fully loaded rig was driven, the VW motor, with its barely 25 HP, had a lot of weight to move. Here the reduction gear of the Kübelwagen was really useful.

The utilitarian vehicles built by the factory in 1945 also included two open types: The Kübelwagen appeared with an open rear bed as Type 27, though only three examples appear to have been built. The Type 81 had a sedan body and was thus a Beetle pickup truck. A great rarity was the VW Type 100, a Beetle with a shortened Kübelwagen chassis, used as a towing tractor.

The 1945-1946 Volkswagens give evidence of the well-developed art of improvisation in those meager years; for the most part, they were assembled in makeshift manner, with poor paint, break-prone steering and pulling brakes normal features in the production of the time. Their equipment was meager; many Beetles have the simple Kübelwagen seats and, to save material, have no door covering, cranked windows or right-side windshield wiper. The single headlights used on Wehrmacht vehicles, supplies of which were still available, were mounted in the front fenders.

Among the test cars were two VW Beetles with four-wheel drive that were built in 1946 of parts left over from Schwimmwagen production. One example remains in the Wolfsburg Auto Museum. It was built in August 1946 and registered on November 27. From the frame number, VR 24 (VR = test frame) it can be deduced that, along with regular production, at least 24 test vehicles, of which nothing else is known, were built.

Efforts were made in 1946 to upgrade and enhance the simple VW sedan somewhat. Thus an early export model was created, with a small amount of chrome (light rings, hubcaps, bumpers and door handles, chromed or painted, differed from car to car), comfortable seats and sometimes gloss paint. A few sporty convertibles were also built. Some of these open Volkswagens, with gray military paint, were used by higher British officers. And Colonel Radclyffe is known to have had a jazzy open two-seater built, which probably was the model for the VW-Hebmüller convertible of 1949-50. Friendly forerunners of the coming Economic Miracle were several VW convertibles with bright two-tone paint and chrome trim.

The year's production for 1946 added up to 10,200 cars. In December the factory had to be shut down for lack of materials. As for the personnel of that era, it might be added that in February the military government named Dr. Münch as Chief Supervisor; his official appointment followed on June 17. On August 31, Münch became General Manager and thus took the place of Rudolf Brömann, who had rubbed the British the wrong way and now departed from the VW works.

# List of Types (August 1945 to October 1946)

(Old type numbers in parentheses)

Type 1    VW Limousine
          Type 10 chassis
          Type 11 two-door sedan (Type 60)
          Type 12 four-door sedan
          Type 13 two-door cabrio-sedan (Type 60 CL)
          Type 14 four-door cabrio-sedan
          Type 15 convertible

Type 2    Kübelwagen
          Type 20 chassis
          Type 21 four-seater (Type 82)
          Type 22 radio vehicle
          Type 23 intelligence vehicle
          Type 24 equipment vehicle
          Type 25 fire vehicle
          Type 26 with starter drive (Type 198)
          Type 27 with pickup body
          Type 28 with box body

Tyoe 3    Kübelwagen with four-wheel drive
          Type 30 chassis
          Type 31 four-seater (Type 86-87)
          Type 32 radio vehicle
          Type 33 intelligence vehicle
          Type 34 equipment vehicle
          Type 35 fire vehicle
          Type 36 with starter drive
          Type 37 with pickup body

Type 4    Large Schwimmwagen
          Type 40 (Type 128)

Type 5    Off-road sedan (high chassis, KdF-Beetle body)
          Type 50 chassis
          Type 51 two-door sedan (Type 92-82 E)
          Type 52 four-door sedan
          Type 53 two-door convertible sedan
          Type 54 four-door convertible sedan
          Type 55 convertible
          Type 56 with large rear bed

Type 6    Stationary motor with regulator
          Type 60 (Type 120)
          Type 61 1500 rpm
          Type 62 1800 rpm
          Type 63 3000 rpm

Type 7    Small Schwimmwagen
          Type 70 (Type 166)

Type 8    Off-road Beetle truck (high chassis)
          Type 80 (= Type 50)
          Type 81 pickup truck

Type 82
Type 83 box van (mail truck)
Type 84: Type 83 with complete luggage rack
Type 85: Type 83 with front luggage rack
Type 86: Type 83 as ambulance
Type 88 fire truck with pump

Type 9    Single-axle Trailer
          Type 91 open trailer
          Type 92/83 box trailer

Type 10   Towing Tractor, shortened Type 20 or 82 chassis
          KdF-Beetle body
          Type 100 on-road towing tractor
          Type 101 two-door pickup truck

British soldiers examine the off-road
Beetle (VW Type 51).

Delivery of off-road Beetles to the British Army in 1945. Note the high-clearance chassis.

British military men at the VW Works for a test ride; behind the two Schwimmwagen is an off-road Beetle (photographed in the summer of 1945).

British officers test a VW Schwimmwagen on the factory grounds and at the nearby Mittelland Canal.

A postwar Kübelwagen, probably built in the summer or fall of 1945, lettered "Wolfsburg Motor Works/ Wolfsburger Motoren Werke" on the door. The hubcaps and right wiper were left off for lack of materials.

Factory grounds, winter 1945-1946, with Kübelwagen, Beetle, Mercedes and Tatra.

A Kübelwagen with box body for the postal system. The first trucks delivered were still Reichspost red; later they were painted yellow. From the summer to the end of 1945, only 275 such Kübelwagen vans (VW Type 28) were built.

An off-road Beetle with box body as an ambulance (VW Type 83). Note the high off-road chassis of the Kübelwagen.

A Reichspost mail van and trailer (1945).

An off-road Beetle with pickup body (1945, with 1948 hubcaps). This was probably a sedan that was later rebuilt into a pickup truck. Below: the same vehicle as a tow car. The off-road chassis with very low gear was particularly suited to that purpose. Therefore these old Beetles were still used at the factory for some years.

The off-road Beetle as a tow car (VW Type 100, 1946), with shortened chassis, Spartan interior with Kübelwagen seats and no door coverings.

The British Army also lost many vehicles in the war. Replacements were urgently needed. Thus the British were happy to put the German Volkswagen into service.

The VW convertible was also requisitioned for military service.

With its two-tone gloss paint and chrome trim, this nice convertible, perhaps rebuilt from a sedan (note rear bodywork over motor hood). The license-plate light is a wartime design. The year it was built is hard to determine; it could be 1944 to 1946-1947. Note the Kübelwagen with wood-gas generator in front of the building in the top photo. Below: in the background are two British army Beetles.

The VW Beetle with normal body was built again in December 1945 in very meager form, as can be seen: no chrome, matte military paint, uniform Wehrmacht headlights (leftover supplies) in the front fenders, also used in the Kübelwagen and trucks (Opel Blitz, Ford 3000 S, Mercedes 4.5-ton). The hubcaps and right windshield wiper were also eliminated. The British occupation forces painted white identification numbers on the front and rear hoods.

Volkswagens for the French Army, sent on their way by rail, summer 1944.

# Postwar Driving

In the first three years after the war, a new car could be bought only with a priority voucher, which were only issued for the privileged few of the occupying powers. The priority-voucher requirement was lifted only a few weeks before the currency reform. Since a new Volkswagen could be purchased regularly only after the summer of 1948, all interested parties in the time just after the war were directed to the used-car market. The VW sedan was very seldom offered for sale there — too few had been built by 1945, and only a few had survived. The 1945-1948 models had almost all been in service with the occupying armies, and such a car was hard to come by. To be sure, on the black market nothing is impossible, and so one might be able to obtain a CCG (Control Commission for Germany) Volkswagen of the Allies from a conniving wheeler-dealer, sly fox or all-out manipulator — naturally at outrageous prices: one had to pay 30,000 to 35,000 RM to such a dealer for an almost-new military VW.

Mustered-out Wehrmacht Kübel- and Schwimmwagen that had survived in what remained of Germany were offered for sale more often than VW Beetles, as they had been built in greater numbers. These reliable off-road vehicles were highly prized by foresters, farmers, repairmen and the like because of their strong traction. And many a one had made a good deal. Whoever was quick and clever and "could hear the grass grow" could obtain such a vehicle for no money at all, for entire Wehrmacht units had disbanded themselves in Bavaria and Austria in May 1945. Their remaining motor vehicles were left standing somewhere at the edge of town or in a green field. Many a person had not waited long to help himself and snap up an ownerless vehicle.

Private customers in the cities preferred to look for a prewar car in good condition, to the extent that their wallets allowed such outrageous luxuries. The prices of used cars climbed to fantastic heights in the time just after the war, for cars were in extremely short supply. If one looks through old newspapers for the fun of it, one can find numerous examples of this: for a still usable 1937-38 Opel Olympia, one had to lay out at least 10,000 to 15,000 RM. Whoever desired a BMW or Mercedes of the same year had to expect to spend 50,000 RM. As for the august brands of Maybach and Horch, one need not even ask. For the people of those days, these were astronomical amounts.

Then too, the buying and selling of motor vehicles included major problems before the currency reform. No car was allowed to change its ownership in one administrative district without the approval of the road traffic officials. And in addition, the vehicle had to be evaluated. The situation with evaluation was that nobody wanted to have it done because the evaluations of the DAT had been set far too low. These evaluations had no practical value, for the sellers demanded the going black-market prices. They had a meaning only in terms of the Reich's financial laws, as regarded compensation and the like.

How, then, could the value of a used car be decided in the chaotic postwar period?

If there were any factors of supply and demand in existence at all, they were those of the dubious black market. The guidelines of the DAT were well-intentioned and sounded convincing, but they had nothing to do with reality:

To evaluate a used car, one started then as now with the price of the new car. But since there were no, or almost no, new cars then, one started with the prewar prices, and after the currency reform, the new value in DM was calculated by adding 80% — much too little, as a look at sales prices will show: in 1938, for example, a four-door Mercedes 170 V cost 3850 Reichsmark, and the same car brought 8180 DM in 1948. For an Opel Olympia, the car that was sold most often before the war, and that more or less represented the bourgeois middle class, the prewar price had been 2675 RM; ten years later it was 6785 DM. The situation was much the same for the Kapitän (3575 RM and 9950 DM) and the "Humpbacked Taunus" (2870 RM and 6695 DM). They were the first models to follow the VW into production in 1947-1948.

As for the defunct makes, those whose manufacturers had been destroyed in the war or given up automobile production afterward (such as Adler or Stoewer), the addition, according to the degree of renown or popularity, sank to some 30%. Naturally the difficulty of obtaining spare parts came into the bargain.

From the calculated maximum value of the vehicle, one then generally subtracted the depreciation on account of age, condition, mileage, etc. The price of used car did, in fact, drop after the currency reform, and one could also begin to buy new cars then. Yet the prices of used cars remained stable. Many people gave preference to a comfortable prewar car over a new VW, for the

VW Standard of 1948 with its Spartan equipment, loudly rattling motor, dull paint, stiff suspension and cable brakes was clearly inferior to the upper-class prewar cars, which obviously had more comfort and engine power. A new Volkswagen cost 5300 DM in 1948; for the same money, one could buy a well-kept Adler Diplomat, BMW, Mercedes or Wanderer after the currency reform.

In those chaotic times, the Volkswagen did have the very valuable advantage of perfectly organized spare-parts supply. No sooner had Heinrich Nordhoff taken command of the VW works than he took every opportunity to remind an eager public of the unparalleled VW customer service. It was an absolute novelty that every authorized VW agency had any desired spare part in stock at any time. From the very start, Nordhoff had invested highly in repair and customer service. And it was true that all parts for the VW were easy to get; even before 1948, when there was no established VW organization, for in Wolfsburg large quantities of automobiles were being produced, and they had to be supplied, as did the numerous Kübelwagen that remained from Wehrmacht stocks.

Otherwise, the spare-parts situation looked worse than miserable. Many cars waited at the repair shops for weeks and months because some essential part was lacking. Naturally, all sorts of tricks were used to improvise and make repairs. Even components that did not belong to the car were used in a pinch. With great improvisational expertise and an absolutely unlimited wealth of inventiveness, the mechanics were able to keep the old cars functioning.

Often, though, the repair shops left the job of finding spare parts up to the helpless customer. The few parts that could still be obtained somewhere with some trouble were usually reserved by the repair-shop people for their own use, or for friends or steady customers. Naturally the possibility of having a part custom-made also existed, but the prices were often more than twenty times the regular price, and thus beyond the customer's ability to pay.

The authorities, the drivers' organizations and the manufacturers tried to counteract the catastrophic situation. The problem, of course, began with that of obtaining materials and the question of what types of vehicles spare parts should be made for. The variety of models, truly incredible in Germany, became even more complicated because, what with the great shortage of usable cars, even the oldest veterans were put back into service. Cars from the 1920s (and even older!) turned up again in road traffic. In the 1920s there had been countless automobile manufacturers in Germany, most of which had disappeared in the 1930s. But from those days of long-gone production, many individual cars were made mobile again after 1945.

In order to use the small stocks of materials sensibly, the existing firms were advised by the military authorities to report which models it was financially worthwhile to make spare parts for. For the purpose of part production, therefore, only such cars that had survived the war in large numbers and in good condition, and thus were still usable for a time, were considered. Rarities and cars 25 or more years old were disqualified as so-called "barred models." The owner of one had no choice but to have parts custom-made if his vehicle was still usable. It also looked bad for vehicles whose production facilities were now in the Russian Zone or in the eastern regions under Polish control. For these manufacturers, "godfather firms" in the western zones were commissioned to make spare parts.

All in all, the supplying of Volkswagen spare parts was truly far and away the best, because the factory in Wolfsburg was already building new cars in 1945, with the other manufacturers following only one or two years later. The repair work done by VW was already in the planning stages before the war, in practice, though, it was trimmed to its most rational form in 1946-1947, being limited to the servicing and repair of only one single type of vehicle. In the autumn of 1945 the customer service department was already being organized at Wolfsburg, with a spare-parts department, a technical department and a customer service school. In February 1946 the first edition of a new spare-parts catalog appeared in German and English (16,000 printed). A second printing followed in September. On October 24, 1947, even before Volkswagens could be sold freely, the spare-parts exchange service began.

Another problem was the shortage of tires.

Even in the Wehrmacht, tire material was running short toward the end of the war, where there was any left. For example, as of 1944, the rear dual wheels of trucks were done away with, as was a second spare wheel. For cars too, whatever tires and wheels were available were used. Meanwhile, four different types of tires (sometimes with different wheel types) were mounted on one car. In the pictures one can see how wretchedly these cars were equipped. And after the war, the situation naturally did not improve for a long time. Since natural rubber was lacking, up to 85% Buna was still used in 1945-1946.

In the British Zone, the use of Buna was reduced to 50% in 1946; in the American Zone, synthetic rubber was still being used to a great extent in 1947.

The result of the use of Buna was an increase in tire temperatures during fairly long trips. In addition, the strength of the walls had to be decreased in order to decrease warmth and friction problems. Attempts were made to counteract the greater weakness of the tires by decreasing top speeds and increasing air pressure.

But that was not enough.

Sufficient quantities of synthetic silk were also lacking; the imported cotton did not live up to the requirements of the tire industry, which was also bothered, just like all other branches of industry during and after the war, by frequent power outages.

Thus the tire industry was nowhere near able to meet the demand. In addition, the general manager of the chief administration of roads stated in a memorandum on the "easing of the tire problem in motor vehicle transport" on June 17, 1947 that the quality of tires and their running performance amounted to only 25 to 30% of their prewar performance.

After the war it was almost impossible to obtain new tires. To be sure, production could be increased rapidly in 1947 (370,000 tires were made by Continental in Hannover), but only a very small percentage could be made available to private drivers; the occupying forces naturally had to be supplied first, then came the German postal system, railways and other government agencies. An additional percentage had to be supplied to the Russian and French Zones. After that, equipping newly-made cars could be considered. At the end of the line were the road traffic authorities, by whom the supplying of spares for the vehicles in use was regulated. And at that point things looked very bad: In the summer of 1948 there were many car owners who, since August 1945, had been allowed only one tire for their vehicles. And this was added to the ruinous condition of the vehicles that had been patched up in makeshift fashion and made usable again: worn-out axle shanks and wheel bearings, a nonstandard track, pulling brakes and the like were completely normal and put more than the usual strain on the weak material of the tires. And since the few vehicles were ruthlessly overloaded on account of the lack of transportation, the results can be imagined. When one also realizes that the German roads and superhighways, what with the results of the war and years without repairs, were in miserable condition and the tire quality was bad because good material could not be had, it is a wonder that a set of tires lasted as long as it did — or had to last. Inner tubes were patched, who knows how many times, and odd-shaped patches were stuck into the tires again and again. New treads were cut into slick, worn-down tires, often only a simple zigzag line two millimeters deep.

Equipped like that, one must have been glad when one could drive thirty kilometers farther without having another flat tire. At the next pothole or sharply projecting paving stone, a trip could come to an abrupt end yet again, and one could speak of luck if he had the necessary articles to trade with him, in order to persuade a grumbling repairman to be somewhat more willing to reach for his patching materials and tools. But many times even the simplest repairing materials were lacking, and even air compressors too.

# Privately Owned Wehrmacht Volkswagens

In the 1950s, the old VW Kübel- and Schwimmwagen were snapped up by private owners who appreciated their reliability and sturdiness. In farming and forestry, the former Wehrmacht Volkswagens were extremely useful. Many owners also sought such a car as a low-priced convertible or camping car. These Volkswagens were also prized for expeditions to Africa, Greece and Turkey. Sometimes the proud owners of these old military vehicles "enhanced" them with extended or modified bodywork, chrome trim or new paint. For example, sometimes a solid roof made by a different company was welded on, or a new body of one's own making was installed. In Czechoslovakia, where the old Wehrmacht Volkswagens had a long life because there was nothing new to replace them, this was a popular method of giving an old car a more modern appearance. One could even encounter a VW Kübel with a Skoda body or a VW-Opel Olympia hybrid. For the sake of simplicity, a car was sometimes repaired by installing a front axle from a VW Beetle, making the Kübelwagen somewhat lower, and doing away with the Schwimmwagen's four-wheel drive.

The VW drivers in the eastern bloc countries in particular made do with such improvisations because there was a lack of original spare parts. Wherever possible, one turned to the local market, for example, for speedometers, headlights, directional and taillights. Among others, the track-rod heads of the Framo delivery truck and the brake lines of the Trabant could be used for conversion to hydraulic brakes.

Naturally, the widespread sales of the Beetle did something else to help the VW owner. In particular, the spare parts of the standard VW (cable brakes, spindle steering, unsynchronized gearbox) could be used in an old Kübelwagen with no problems.

Without a doubt, the owners of the veteran Volkswagens were great car builders in the eyes of the Lord — with a small workshop and an assortment of spare parts in the cellar, barn or garage, and naturally with a wealth of experience. Many of them remained true to their old Kübelwagen for a number of years, even for decades. The car accompanied them on many a trip for almost a lifetime.

Most of the Wehrmacht Volkswagens, though, were ruthlessly scrapped, left to stand and rust or simply thrown away in the 1950s and 1960s. Many an old Kübel landed in a gravel pit, a bomb crater or a garbage dump that was later filled in. Sometimes the worn-out car was simply shoved into a lake. And often enough, an old Volkswagen ended its days in the bushes at the edge of a forest, where it rusted away over the years until only an overgrown frame remained, which finally fell to pieces. In the "Golden West", which developed into a consumer society at the end of the 1950s, nobody had any use for a wretched old tin box with pulling brakes, steering that was far from play-free, a troublesome, unsynchronized gearbox, a stiff suspension, too much noise and too little heat. The masses of the motor-hungry Germans oriented themselves to the newest products.

The last cars of the 1940s disappeared from the streets in the period from about 1958 to 1963. After ten to twenty years of service, almost all of them were scrapped. Buyers could be found only among do-it-yourselfers and students, where such an old car, often enough a convertible from the 1930s, would sell for 200 to 300 Marks. For many, the parting was not easy. Who wants to part with a loyal old comrade with which one has covered many thousands of kilometers? As long as everything went well, the decision could be put off, but one days the signs of age made themselves felt clearly. The motor no longer provided full power, the brakes had to be redone, the gearbox or differential rattled, the clutch slipped. One had to accept a general overhaul — but what might it cost? Night after night was spent calculating until the decision to buy a new car was finally made. But it was not so easy to get rid of the old car. The veterans of the 1930s and 1940s had no antique or museum value around 1960, and they stood alone and unloved in the back corner of the used-car dealer's lot. Chromed, high-powered modern cars were the thing. Who wanted such an old mouse-gray thing to ruin his reputation?

Only toward the end of the 1960s did the old wartime Volkswagen begin to take on the character of an enthusiast's car. A small group of enthusiasts had already taken an interest in the Schwimmwagen a few years earlier. The parts supply was organized systematically, soon a first meet was organized and a club was formed. Kübelwagen prices remained reasonable a little longer, for there were more of them around. A sturdy Kübel with TUV could still be bought for 1000 to 2000 DM around 1968. Only at the beginning of the 1970s did the growing popularity of oldtimers bring about a rapid rise in prices and a flourishing market.

Unfortunately, the scene now lost much of the initial originality that the passionate motorists had given it. The Schwimmwagen in particular grew into a prestige car and status symbol, and thus all too often an arrogant, elitist clique showed up at the meets, making a stupid spectacle of itself with all its excesses.

Most of the vehicles were still restored authentically, with a lot of time and money expended. A few VW enthusiasts even built replicas of the "War Beetle." In fact, only very few of the VW Type 82 E that one sees today are original. Many of these cars have a newer VW body (up to 1952) on the Kübel chassis, or sometimes only Kübel axles. Even just a couple axle shanks of the Kübelwagen and a rear axle from an old VW Bus are enough to turn a Beetle into what appears to be a Wehrmacht VW. Now and then in more recent times, a 4wd Beetle turns up here and there, rebuilt with parts from a Schwimmwagen. All of this is naturally very costly and scarcely within the reach of the typical workingman.

Whoever is looking for a low-priced old Kübel nowadays, though, does not need to give up in despair. After the opening of the Eastern Bloc, an old Wehrmacht VW has been offered for sale now and then. One must know, though, that vehicles from those countries are thoroughly worn out as a rule. But the VW 181 can still be bought cheaply from the Bundeswehr. This new version of the old Kübelwagen corresponds thoroughly to the characteristics of the original, and has the added advantage for the newcomer of being a practical everyday car, thanks to its modern technology.

A scrap heap of stacked-up Kübelwagen bod-
ies. On either side of the DKW are parts of a
VW Schwimmwagen. Photographed near
Braunschweig, probably in 1948.

A repair-shop yard with vehicles to be repaired. A Kübelwagen is on blocks with its wheels removed. Behind it is a VW Beetle with box body.

A repair-shop crew with their Kübelwagen, an especially good tow car because of its low gears.

A worn-out Kübelwagen with wood-gas generator; it probably came from Reichspost stocks and formerly had a box body.

An ex-Reichspost Beetle, as can be seen by the off-road chassis.

The front of this Kübel-
wagen has been raised
by a hood, with the
spare wheel on top of it

This VW Kübel had a hard life in Czech hands, as can be seen by all its rebuilding. Even the axles and wheels are not original.

Old military Beetles were scrapped at this junkyard.

This well-preserved, well-kept old Kübel was used regularly for years in Czechoslovakia.

The VW Kübel helps harvest the hay.

On a vacation trip in Greece!

This amphibian was decorated for a garden show in 1955.

Campers with VW Schwimmwagen on the Neckar, the Model and near Bingen.

A Kübelwagen carries a Schwimmwagen body piggyback.

Found in Italy in the 1970s: a streamlined ex-VW Schwimmwagen.

Electioneering with a Kübelwagen, 1949.

Old Wehrmacht Kübelwagen were often turned into "limousines" through remarkable rebuilding. This one was seen in Crete around 1978.

In the 1950s, several old Wehrmacht VW's were used in war and homeland films. Above: a scene from "Operation Sleeping Bag"; below: "The First Day of Freedom" (1964), a film made by Polish director and Soviet prize-winner Aleksander Ford.

A jewel: This old Wehrmacht VW was fancied up with chromed bumpers, grille and gleaming hubcaps, stylish paint, whitewall tires and a flashy rack on the front. The spare tire cover and roof are made of black-painted fabric. On the grille is a vase with flowers, plus a dying swan. Whether one considers it beautiful is another matter. Photographed on a parking lot at Old Mythenae in the Argolis, 1958.

This ugly plastic copy was offered by a Kaiserslautern firm in the late 1970s, as a kit without the Beetle chassis for 4500 DM, or complete for 10,300 DM.

A VW 82 of 1941 with short rear fenders and no jack opening (before chassis number 8501), in dark green Wehrmacht paint.

This Kübelwagen, chassis number 2 032 217, was built on November 29, 1943 and delivered to the Army Equipment Office in Erfurt. After the war it was used until 1964, painted red, by the volunteer firemen of Kötzing in the Bavarian Forest.

A VW 166 of 1944 parked beside a Churchill-Avre in Graye sur Marne, Normandy. The Churchill was underground for 35 years after falling into a pit of water, was then hauled out and restored externally.

This four-wheel-drive Beetle was rebuilt in original form. The chassis dates from 1944, the body from about 1950. The car was sold by a Norwegian to a German in 1992 and now belongs to a collector in Lorch, Württemberg.

The two original VW's, the Beetle and the Kübelwagen, were used in goodly numbers by the Bundeswehr and, for example, also by the armies of Holland, Belgium and Switzerland. The Beetle shown here is a VW 1200 of 1977, used by a Luftwaffe communications unit in Karlsruhe.

The VW Kübel 181 in civilian form: There were very few customers for the new version in Germany, but a large market in the USA. German customers included the Border Patrol, postal system, Technische Hilfswerke and fire departments.

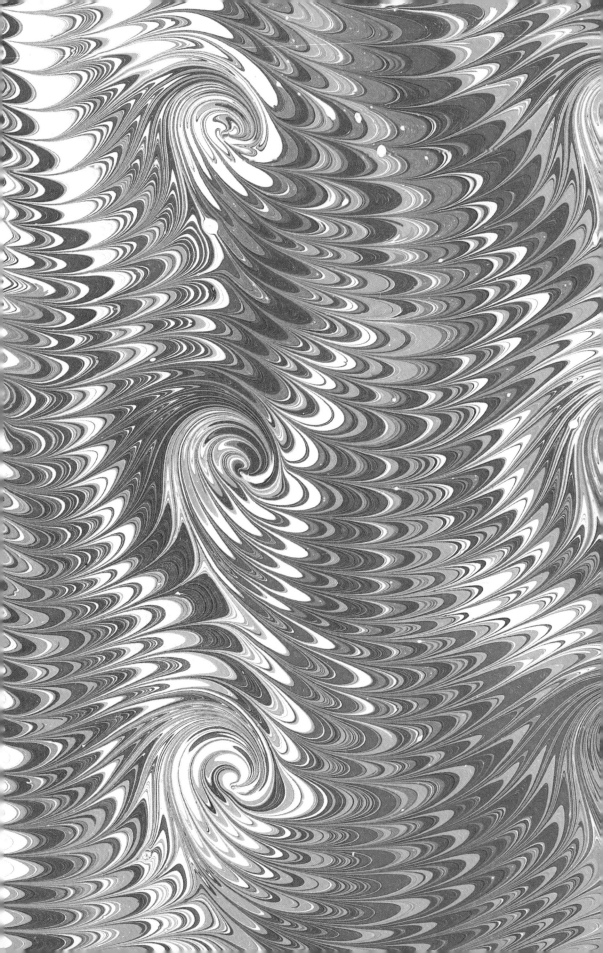